my **revision** n

AQA GCSE
CITIZENSHIP
STUDIES

Mike Mitchell

HODDER
EDUCATION
AN HACHETTE UK COMPANY

Acknowledgements

The Publishers would like to thank the following for permission to reproduce copyright material:

p. 73 Extract from *The Magazine for Prisoners*,
www.insidetime.org/articleview.asp?a=755&c=the_criminal_justice_system_in_a_nutshell

Every effort has been made to trace all copyright holders, but if any have been inadvertently overlooked the Publishers will be pleased to make the necessary arrangements at the first opportunity.

Although every effort has been made to ensure that website addresses are correct at time of going to press, Hodder Education cannot be held responsible for the content of any website mentioned in this book. It is sometimes possible to find a relocated web page by typing in the address of the home page for a website in the URL window of your browser.

Hachette UK's policy is to use papers that are natural, renewable and recyclable products and made from wood grown in sustainable forests. The logging and manufacturing processes are expected to conform to the environmental regulations of the country of origin.

Orders: please contact Bookpoint Ltd, 130 Milton Park, Abingdon, Oxon OX14 4SB. Telephone: (44) 01235 827720. Fax: (44) 01235 400454. Lines are open 9.00–5.00, Monday to Saturday, with a 24-hour message answering service. Visit our website at www.hoddereducation.co.uk

Cover photo: Social network © browndogstudios/istockphoto.com
Illustrations by Datapage and Nomad Graphique
Typeset in Cronos Pro 11.5 points by Datapage India Pvt Ltd
Printed in India
A catalogue record for this title is available from the British Library
ISBN: 978 1444 154 788

Get the most from this book

This book will help you revise for the AQA GCSE Citizenship Short Course and Full Course specifications (examination Unit 1 and Unit 3). It is essential to review your work, learn it and test your understanding. Tick each box when you have:

- revised and understood a topic
- tested yourself and practised the exam questions.

☑ **Tick to track your progress**

Use the revision planner on pages 4–7 to plan your revision, topic by topic.

You can also keep track of your revision by ticking off each topic heading throughout the book. You may find it helpful to add your own notes as you work through each topic.

T1 Community Action and Active Citizenship

		Revised	Tested
1.1	**What factors make for effective 'active citizenship'?**		
15	The tactics of pressure group campaigns		
17	Target groups		
18	Case studies: campaigns to secure rights		
19	Recent UK-based case studies of campaigning		

U1 The tactics of pressure group campaigns   Revised ☐

Pressure groups use a wide variety of methods in order to promote their campaigns.

- **Petitions** – collections of signatures indicating support for an agreed statement. These are used to show the strength of
- **Boycotts** – deciding not to purchase certain goods or services because of a particular cause. The original term related

Features to help you succeed

U1 Short Course

If you are doing the Short Course, you only need to cover the Unit 1 material, shown in the topic heading as U1.

U3 Full Course

If you are doing the Full Course, you should also cover the Unit 3 material, shown in the topic heading as U3.

Key terms

Key terms from the specification are shown at the start of each topic.

Remember

These provide key points to remember for each topic in the exams.

Examiner tip

Throughout the book there are exam tips that explain how you can boost your final grade.

Websites

Carry out some further research and make sure you have the up-to-date information and knowledge to take into the exam.

Test yourself

Use these questions at the end of each Unit 1 section to make sure that you have understood every topic. Check your answers at the back of this book on pages 102–04.

Exam practice

Practice exam questions are provided for each topic. Use them to consolidate your revision and practise your exam skills.

Go online

Go online at **www.therevisionbutton.co.uk/ myrevisionnotes** to find answers to the practice exam questions and try out the quick quizzes.

Contents and revision planner

	Short course topics	Full course topics

T1 Community Action and Active Citizenship

T2 Being a Citizen in the UK: Democracy and Identity

T2 — Being a Citizen in the UK: Democracy and Identity

T2   Being a Citizen in the UK: Democracy and Identity

T3   Fairness and Justice

Revised   Tested

What is Citizenship about?

What does Citizenship mean?

The terms 'citizens' and 'citizenship' are used in everyday language, yet as a compulsory school subject in the UK, Citizenship is relatively new.

In it simplest meaning, citizenship is about belonging. Having citizenship grants an individual an identity and a sense of belonging. With that belonging come both rights as a citizen and responsibilities.

What is the study of Citizenship about?

The study of Citizenship is about the knowledge associated with being a citizen in the UK. This means having an understanding of the concepts associated with citizenship. It also means having an understanding of the necessary skills and processes needed to become an active participating citizen within contemporary UK society, who, if they wish, can try to make a difference in their community or society as a whole.

What is covered in the study of Citizenship?

Considering the very broad nature of citizenship, a whole range of other subjects and topics are referred to when studying Citizenship in the UK: rights and responsibilities, fairness and justice link to issues relating to law and the social structure of society; democracy links to politics; identity links to demography and culture; global problems and issues link to topics like human rights and how we now live in what is called a 'global village', where what happens in another part of the globe can impact upon our lives in the UK.

As well as a body of information, which is constantly being updated, Citizenship as a subject is about enabling you to become empowered and be an active member of society. A wide range of transferable skills is required when considering Citizenship issues. You need to develop a critical mind to be able to weigh up evidence to make judgements, develop arguments, sustain points and reach conclusions based upon evidence.

Why study Citizenship?

Citizenship is not just about studying books or doing internet research, it is also about developing skills and an understanding of the processes needed by a citizen in the twenty-first century to be able, if they wish, to participate fully in society, to become an active citizen who can try to make a difference.

The structure of the AQA GCSE Citizenship Studies course encourages the development of your citizenship knowledge and understanding, but also seeks to develop the skills you need to become an active participating citizen.

GCSE Citizenship, as well as being a useful subject in its own right, helps prepare you for a broad range of post-16 courses, including A level Citizenship Studies.

What are the needs of the AQA specification?

How is the specification organised?

The AQA specification is organised into four themes:

1. Community Action and Active Citizenship
2. Being a Citizen in the UK: Democracy and Identity
3. Fairness and Justice
4. Global Issues and Making a Difference.

Each theme covers a broad area of citizenship. Some of the content from one theme can assist you when you are studying another theme. The content of the Short Course (Unit 1) covers the requirements of the National Programme of Study for Citizenship at Key Stage 4. The content of the Full Course (Unit 3) seeks to extend and add further depth. The two courses should be seen as overlapping, with the Short Course as a precursor to the Full Course.

Short Course	Full Course

How does the assessment work?

GCSE Citizenship Studies has two assessment components:

● written examination papers
● controlled assessment.

Short Course

The Short Course is made up of:
● **Unit 1:** Written Paper – worth **40 per cent** of the total Short Course award
● **Unit 2:** Controlled Assessment – worth **60 per cent** of the total Short Course award.

Full Course

In order to achieve a full GCSE, you are required to take two further units, so that you take four in total.
● **Unit 1**: Written Paper – worth **20 per cent** of the total Full Course award.
● **Unit 2:** Controlled Assessment – worth **30 per cent** of the total Full Course award.
● **Unit 3:** Written Paper – worth **20 per cent** of the total Full Course award.
● **Unit 4:** Controlled Assessment – worth **30 per cent** of the total Full Course award.

Controlled Assessment

● **Unit 2:** The task for the Short Course is called Advocacy and Representation. It is about convincing others that action needs taking about a topic you have researched. This involves you undertaking work on your own or with others, and writing up an account under semi-examination conditions in your school.

● **Unit 4:** The task for the Full Course is called Taking Informed and Responsible Action. This can be based upon the work you undertook for the short course Controlled Assessment, or it could be a new task. It is about taking informed and responsible action to bring about change.

The Controlled Assessment tasks you undertake **must** be chosen from a list that AQA prescribes. The Controlled Assessment element is completed prior to the written paper, so you must ensure that you do well in this if you want to get a good grade.

Schools initially mark the Controlled Assessment tasks then external AQA moderators check the marking. The written examination papers are marked externally by AQA examiners.

How the AQA Citizenship specification is organised

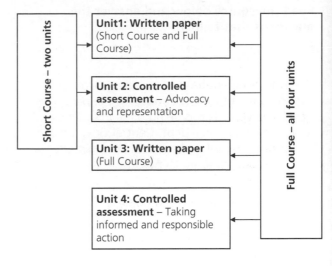

Guide to the Short Course Exam

The written examination paper for the GCSE Short Course Citizenship Studies is one hour in length. It is worth 40 per cent of the total Short Course award and 20 per cent of the total Full Course award. The exam paper is marked out of a total of 40 marks.

The paper is divided into Section A and Section B.

Section A

Section A of the Short Course paper is made up of two questions, both of which are compulsory. All the questions in Section A are based only upon Theme 1: Community Action and Active Citizenship. You should spend approximately 30 minutes answering the questions in this section. There are 20 marks available for Section A.

Question 1 has ten questions worth one mark each.

a) What is a petition?   *(1 mark)*

These are short response questions, which sometimes can be answered in a few words. The question is only worth one mark so it is looking for one clear point – avoid writing too much as you can't gain an extra mark. These questions often use the 'trigger words' (what you have to do): 'identify' or 'name', 'outline' or 'give an example'.

Question 2 is a three-part question worth ten marks in total.

Part a) is worth 3 marks, part b) is worth 3 marks and part c) is worth 4 marks. These questions are based on source material that can be presented as written text, tables, charts or data.

Read the source below and answer the questions that follow.

Source A

The Government has instructed all local councils to cut their spending for the next year by 15 percent. This is being done in order to cut the current national debt. Central Government and the devolved bodies are also required to cut their spending by 15 percent.

a) Identify three devolved bodies in the UK. *(3 marks)*

b) How might the proposed cuts affect local services? *(3 marks)*

c) Outline how else the Government might cut the national debt other than by cutting government spending. *(4 marks)*

Both 3-mark questions require three pieces of information or examples to gain full marks. Parts a) and b) require short sentence responses identifying three points or a short paragraph which contains three points. Part c), the 4-mark question, requires a short piece of extended writing, approximately six to eight lines of text. Remember that this question is unseen but must be based on Theme 1 of the specification.

Section B

Section B of the Short Course written paper is made up of three questions. You are only required to answer **one** of these questions. You should spend approximately 30 minutes answering the questions in this section. There are 20 marks available for Section B.

- **One question** is based on Theme 2: Being a Citizen in the UK: Democracy and Identity.
- **One question** is based on Theme 3: Fairness and Justice.
- **One question** is based on Theme 4: Global Issues and Making a Difference.

The titles of the topics on which the questions are based are pre-released each year by AQA, so that you can do some in-depth preparation for your chosen topic. For example, the topics could be pre-released as:

Question 3 – Identity and Democracy: Voting

Question 4 – Fairness and Justice: Anti-social Behaviour

Question 5 – Global Issues and Making a Difference: Poverty and Fair Trade

Each of the questions in Section B follows the same structure. Part a) is worth 2 marks, part b) is worth 6 marks and part c) is worth 12 marks. These questions are based on unseen source material, which can be presented as written text, tables, charts or data.

3 Read the source below and answer parts a), b) and c) which follow.

Source A

Scotland to leave the UK
Leading pollsters are predicting that in the forthcoming referendum on Scottish independence, 53 per cent will vote for full independence for Scotland. It is estimated that only 40 percent of voters will turn out to vote. The UK Prime Minister has stated that he is opposed to Scotland withdrawing from the Union, as have the leaders of all the major UK parties. The leader of the Scottish Parliament has said that what is important is the will of the people of Scotland and the UK Parliament should not try to block Scottish independence.

a) What do you understand by the term 'the Union'? *(2 marks)*

b) Briefly outline the case a UK prime minister could make to the people of Scotland to vote 'no' in the referendum. *(6 marks)*

c) What are the advantages for Scotland if it gained full independence? *(12 marks)*

Part a) responses require two pieces of information. Each point made should be no longer than a single sentence. If the trigger word is 'name' or 'identify', a single word or phrase is sufficient. If the trigger is 'outline', then one or two sentences may be required.

Part b) normally requires three pieces of evidence with some supporting comment. You gain a mark for identification and one for extension. The trigger may be 'briefly outline' which means give the main points with some elaboration – you only have twelve lines to complete, so no introduction is required, just answer the question as stated. No conclusion is required.

Part c) is a short essay and should follow a structure; opening statement, main evidence and lastly a brief conclusion. This part is worth 12 marks. If you are asked to make a case or present an argument you may only be required to give a response from one point of view. If you are required to give both sides of an argument this will be indicated in the question and that part will be in bold text. If the response only requires one point of view, indicate in the conclusion that there are other views on this matter – this shows understanding of the issue. Remember that the topic title is pre-released to help you research the topic. If the topic pre-release contains three phrases, remember that there are three questions to answer.

GCSE Short Course

Unit 1 (1 hour) – maximum mark is 40. Summary of question types

Section A – You must answer **all** these questions.

1   Ten parts each worth one mark and requiring short answers.   *(10 marks)*

2   a) Requires three short points.   *(3 marks)*

b) Requires three short points.   *(3 marks)*

c) Present a case or make an argument, approx. six- to eight-line answer.   *(4 marks)*

Section B – You must answer **one** question, either Question 3, 4 or 5. The topics are pre-released.

3–5 Based on unseen source material.

a) Identify two points.   *(2 marks)*

b) Extended writing of 12 to 16 lines.   *(6 marks)*

c) Short essay of 25 to 33 lines.   *(12 marks)*

Guide to the Full Course exam

The written examination paper for the GCSE Full Course Citizenship Studies is one hour in length. It is worth 20 per cent of the total Full Course award. The exam paper is marked out of a total of 40 marks.

The paper is divided into Section A and Section B.

Section A

Section A of the Full Course written paper is made up of four questions. You are required to answer all four questions. You should spend approximately 30 minutes answering the questions in this section.

There are 20 marks available for Section A. Each of the questions in Section A is based on the themes from the specification.

- **One question** is based on Theme 1: Community Action and Active Citizenship.

- **One question** is based on Theme 2: Being a Citizen in the UK: Democracy and Identity.

- **One question** is based on Theme 3: Fairness and Justice.

- **One question** is based on Theme 4: Global Issues and Making a Difference.

Each of the questions in Section A follows the same structure and is worth 5 marks in total. Part a) is worth 1 mark, part b) is worth 2 marks and part c) is worth 2 marks. These questions are based on unseen source material, which can be presented as written text, tables, charts or data.

Read the source below and answer parts a), b) and c) which follow.

Source A

Global Crisis
In 2008, there was a global financial crisis caused by bank lending to people who could not repay their debts. Several major investment firms and US banks failed and this triggered banking problems worldwide. In 2011, there is concern about the ability of some countries to repay their debts and they are being forced to reduce their spending and raise taxes.

a) Identify one international body that is involved in trying to help countries that have problems with their debts.   *(1 mark)*

b) Explain one impact on ordinary citizens of the global banking crisis.   *(2 marks)*

c) What is the role of the G8 in relation to this global crisis?   *(2 marks)*

The sources for these questions may give an answer to a question or just provide some ideas or help give you some thoughts about the questions. Part a) just requires a short response and may use trigger words like 'identify', 'name', 'give an example of'. Parts b) and c) may require two pieces of information or one fact supported by some evidence. The trigger words could be 'explain' or 'outline briefly'.

Remember to read the source before answering the questions. If you find one question difficult, move on to the next and come back to any missing questions later.

Section B

Section B of the Full Course written paper is made up of three questions. You are only required to answer **one** question. You should spend approximately 30 minutes answering the questions in this section. There are 20 marks available for Section B.

- **One question** is based on Theme 2: Being a Citizen in the UK: Democracy and Identity.

- **One question** is based on Theme 3: Fairness and Justice.

- **One question** is based on Theme 4: Global Issues and Making a Difference.

The titles of the topics on which the questions are based are pre-released each year by AQA, so that you can do some in-depth preparation on your chosen topic. For example, the topics could be pre-released as:

- **Question 5** – Fairness and Justice: The Prison System

- **Question 6** – Community Action and Active Citizenship: The Media

- **Question 7** – Global Issues and Making a Difference: International Conflict

Each of the questions in Section B follows the same structure. Part a) is worth 2 marks, part b) is worth 6 marks and part c) is worth 12 marks. These questions are based on unseen source material, which can be presented as written text, tables, charts or data. This question type is identical to those for the Short Course Section B (see page 10), except that here the source appears after part a) and links to part b) that follows.

Pre-released topic: Being a Citizen in the UK: Immigration

> a) Explain what is meant by the term 'immigration'. *(2 marks)*
>
> **Read the source below and answer part b) which follows.**
>
> Source A
>
> **The Effects of Immigration**
> Many people are concerned about the high levels of people coming into the UK in recent years. Many complain that they take employment away from British workers. Others welcome people from other countries and many employers claim they do jobs that UK citizens refuse to do and without these workers many businesses would not survive.
>
> b) Explain two ways in which immigrants aid the UK economy. *(6 marks)*
>
> c) Present a case for controlling the number of immigrants that come to the UK. Why might some people disagree? *(12 marks)*

GCSE Full Course

Unit 3 (1 hour) – maximum mark is 40. Summary of question types

Section A – You must answer **all** these questions.

1–4 Based on unseen source material.
a) Requires a short answer. *(1 mark)*
b) Requires a short answer. *(2 marks)*
c) Requires a short answer. *(2 marks)*

Section B – You must answer **one** question: either Question 5, 6 or 7. The topics are pre-released.

5–7 a) Short response up to four lines. *(2 marks)*
b) Extended writing of 12 to 16 lines. *(6 marks)*
c) Short essay of 25 to 33 lines. *(12 marks)*

Countdown to my exams

6–8 weeks to go

- Gather all your Citizenship material in one place, such as a file or box. Include: any textbooks that you have; your written work from your Citizenship lessons and homework; any past examination materials you have been given (question papers and mark schemes, examiner reports and the details of the pre-released topics – all available to centres from the AQA website, www.aqa.org.uk); any teacher handouts you have been given; research materials, such as notes from the internet, or resource materials you have found, especially in relation to the pre-released topics for the Short and Full Course written papers; a copy of the specification; this revision guide.

- Sort your materials into the four themes of the specification. Add tabs to any textbooks using colour-coded sticky notes.

- Start by looking at the teaching specifications. Look through your materials for Theme 1 and make sure you have covered everything on the specification. The revision planner on pages 4–7 will help you to group your notes into topics. This is the most important theme as you have to answer all the questions.

- Go to the theme you have selected for Part B of the examination paper and check your materials against the teaching specification for that theme. You could keep the material for that theme in a separate file.

- Work out a realistic revision plan to complete your revision. Plan gaps to give yourself a rest and to give you extra time in case you miss any of your planned revision slots. Do not plan to continually revise one subject for days on end – make sure you alternate subjects.

- Set yourself sensible targets. Break your revision down into focused sessions of around 40 minutes, divided by breaks. These Revision Notes organise the basic facts into short, memorable sections to make revising easier.

Revised ☐

4–6 weeks to go

- Read through the relevant sections of this book and refer to the examiner tips, remember boxes and key terms. Tick off the topics as you feel confident about them. Highlight those topics you find difficult and look at them again in detail. Remember to have the AQA pre-release topic sheet with you when you revise the topic you have selected from Section B.

- Learn the key terms at the start of each topic in this book. To show clear understanding of the term, write an example next to each one. If possible, make the example recent and UK-based.

- Test your understanding of each topic by working through the Test yourself questions in the book. Look up the answers at the back of the book.

- Make a note of any problem areas as you revise and ask your teacher to go over these in class.

- Look at past papers. They are one of the best ways to revise and practise your exam skills. Write or prepare planned answers to the exam practice questions provided in this book. Check your answers online and try out the quick quizzes at **www.therevisionbutton.co.uk/myrevisionnotes**

- Try different revision methods. Make notes as you revise – you could use mind maps and spider diagrams. Create your own flash cards with questions from past papers on one side and information in bullet points on the other.

- Track your progress using the revision planner and give yourself a reward when you have achieved your target.

Revised ☐

Countdown to my exams

One week to go

- Try to fit in at least one more timed practice of an entire past paper and seek feedback from your teacher, comparing your work closely with the mark scheme.

- Check the revision planner to make sure you haven't missed any topics. Brush up on any areas of difficulty by talking them over with a friend or getting help from your teacher.

- Attend any revision classes put on by your teacher. Remember, he or she is an expert at preparing people for examinations.

Revised ☐

The day before the examination

- Flick through these Revision Notes for Theme 1 and for the themes that you will be answering questions on in Section B.

- Look again at the AQA pre-release topic sheet for the topic you have selected from Section B.

- Check the time and place of your examination.

- Make sure you have everything you need – extra pens and pencils, tissues, a watch, bottled water, sweets.

- Allow some time to relax and have an early night to ensure you are fresh and alert for the examination.

Revised ☐

My exams

GCSE Citizenship Studies Short Course: Unit 1

Date: ....

Time: ....

Location: ....

GCSE Citizenship Studies Full Course: Unit 3

Date: ....

Time: ....

Location: ....

In the examination

Clearly, knowing the answers is key to any examination success! There is nothing worse for the examiner than marking vague, general responses that do not relate to the question.

Here are some suggestions on how to improve your performance in the exam.

- At the start, quickly read the paper once through. If you feel that you can answer the Section B question well, complete it before the Section A questions. Remember to allow 30 minutes per section.

- If you are uncertain about an answer, leave it and come back to it later.

- Section A question 1 in Unit 1 requires short answers only. Don't panic if you don't know the answer as each question is only one mark. Remember to read the question carefully – what does it want you to do? Look for the trigger word in Section A question 1 such as 'name', 'identify', 'give an example' – all require you to identify something. Remember to use an example to show your understanding.

- Questions that involve source material encourage you to use the source, but they expect you to be able to add your own knowledge to the material contained in the source if you want to gain higher marks.

- Read the question carefully to identify your task for the higher mark questions. Is it to write a case for and against or to present only one side? If both are required, ensure you write about the same amount for each side. You are not asked directly for your opinions, so you should refer to evidence and, if required, draw a conclusion based upon the evidence you have presented.

- Ensure that any case studies or examples used are up to date.

- Try to allow yourself five minutes at the end of the examination to read through your paper to correct any errors.

Revised ☐

1.1 What factors make for effective 'active citizenship'?

Key terms

Being an active citizen – having the knowledge, skills and understanding to participate in society and the ability to try to bring about change.

Campaigning – an organised series of events and activities that seek to influence the views of others.

Community action – citizens within a local community coming together in regards to an issue, or working together to bring about change within the community. This could be as an informal group or as part of an organised body.

Democracy – a society where citizens, through an open and fair electoral system, are able to vote in regular elections. It is where a range of different political ideas are allowed, where governments are accountable, and there is a respect for human rights and a 'free press' – a press not restricted or controlled by the Government.

Direct action – campaigning that can include non-violent or violent activities, which target persons, groups or property deemed offensive to the protester.

Freedom (of association, of speech, the vote) – the ability to be able to act in a certain way without interference. Used in a citizenship context in regard to rights as a citizen, i.e. freedom of association – to be able to meet freely with others without fear of persecution.

Indirect action – campaigning that can include support for a group, signing petitions or lobbying on behalf of a pressure group.

Participation – taking part in civic society through formal processes such as voting or standing for election, or informal actions such as volunteering or joining community groups.

Pressure groups – groups of citizens normally linked together into formal groups who share the same view regarding bringing about change. Some groups wish to maintain the current situation or protect the interests of a specific group.

U1 The tactics of pressure group campaigns

Revised

Pressure groups use a wide variety of methods in order to promote their campaigns.

- **Petitions** – collections of signatures indicating support for an agreed statement. These are used to show the strength of support for the statement.

- **Leafleting** – distributing materials that support a particular point of view, often asking for support and/or financial help.

- **Media promotion** – staging events and protests to attract media attention and publicity.

- **Boycotts** – deciding not to purchase certain goods or services because of a particular cause. The original term related to Captain Boycott, an Irish landowner whose tenants refused to pay their rent.

- **Use of celebrity** – by attracting celebrities, support groups are often able to gain media coverage and boost the number of their supporters.

- **Lobbying** – a general term about making your views known to those whose opinions you wish to influence. The specific term relates to citizens approaching their Member of Parliament (MP) to raise an issue. This is done in the Lobby of the House of Commons.

- **Professional lobbying** – wealthier pressure groups and other bodies employ professional lobbyists. These are full-time employed people who work for commercial bodies whose job is to approach those they wish to influence and present the case for the group that employs them.

- **Demonstrations** – these can take many forms, from small groups to mass marches and rallies.

- **Direct action** – this can take either a non-violent or violent form. Non-violent examples include strikes, occupation of buildings and sit-ins. Violent direct action includes destroying property, assault and rioting. The term 'civil disobedience' also relates to direct action. This normally involves citizens disobeying rules or laws with which they disagree.

- **Use of e-media** – this format of campaigning has become increasingly important. E-media enables groups to contact their supporters quickly, give them the latest information and correct any media stories. It also enables groups to quickly contact the traditional media (newspapers and television).

Examiner tip

When studying for this topic, it is helpful to be able to use recent local or national examples of pressure group methods. It is also relevant to use examples in which you have been involved – for example, signing a petition at school.

Possible changes

Major changes are taking place due to the influence of e-media: internet, social networks, messaging services and Twitter. All these allow information and messages to be passed to supporters and the traditional media far more rapidly. We now live in a 24/7 news culture and this means there is an appetite for news, events and activities. E-media also means that those in power are more accessible than before. Many politicians have blogs and Twitter accounts and respond to events as they occur. In 2011, the Government introduced the idea of online e-petitions whereby if 100,000 citizens signed an online petition, the House of Commons would debate the issue.

Websites

This website brings together a range of protest and pressure groups and enables citizens to take part in their campaigns: www.38degrees.org.uk

Examiner tip

To prepare for the exam, focus on a few examples of pressure groups that operate in different ways.

Pressure group	Methods
Amnesty International www.amnesty.org.uk	Asks members to write to governments in support of 'prisoners of conscience' to campaign for their release. A 'prisoner of conscience' is a person who is held in confinement by their government because they wish to utilise basic human rights, i.e. the right to vote or protest.
RSPCA www.rspca.org.uk	Uses the media to highlight campaigns and seek financial help to support its work.
Greenpeace www.greenpeace.org.uk	Takes direct non-violent action to promote its cause.
Stop the War Coalition www.stopwar.org.uk	Uses lobbying and mass demonstrations to seek to influence politicians.

Revise a range of different pressure groups, including local, national and international, which cover a range of issues and methods of working. Record the information in a table like the one above. Look at the websites of the pressure groups prior to the exam to keep up to date with their campaigns.

In order to bring about change, a pressure group must first decide who or what it wishes to influence. It needs to think about the people or the organisation that has to make or change a decision to bring about what is wanted. That is the target group for pressure group action. In the exam, you will need to use contemporary examples to support your answers to questions about target groups.

Local community examples

School uniform policy

You wish to change the school uniform policy at your school. First, you may wish to get the school council on your side to prove you have the support of other students. Does the head teacher support your views? How do you influence the school's governing body, which will make any final decision? Although the governors are the major targets, the school council and the head teacher are important targets en route to achieving your aim.

Local youth centre

You wish to keep open a local youth centre threatened with closure. Your target group is the local council that made the initial decision to close it. The other target groups could be local councillors, fellow young people and adults and the local media, all of whom could assist you in applying pressure on the local council.

Animal testing

You may disagree with animal testing for beauty products or the use of fur in clothing, and therefore your target groups might include local shops, national retail chains, the product manufacturers and the media. You may include politicians if you want a change in the law.

The target group relates to the change you wish to bring about. You also need to think about the nature of the change. Do you just want to raise awareness of an issue? If so, the media is an important factor. Or do you want a specific change that is feasible to carry out when media interest may not actually aid your cause?

Examiner tip

When revising it is important to think of two different target groups: those that can **bring about the change themselves** and those that can **influence others** who can make the change.

Examiner tip

When answering a question, remember to think about what the aim of the example campaign is, as that can determine the types and number of target groups. There may be more than one target group that you wish to influence. Is the media always the best way of promoting your cause?

Examiner tip

Remember this part of the course with these three questions:

- What is the name of the pressure group?
- What are they trying to achieve?
- Who do they need to influence (target groups)?

1.1 What factors make for effective 'active citizenship'?

U1 Case studies: campaigns to secure rights

Revised

Case study: votes for women in the twentieth century

Various groups within the female suffrage movement used a range of campaigning methods. The suffragettes, associated with Mrs Pankhurst, used direct action which involved illegal activities to promote their cause while other groups campaigning to get women the vote used peaceful methods. The role of women during the First World War changed many people's attitudes to women gaining the vote. Women aged over 28 were given the vote in 1918. Universal suffrage (the right to vote) was granted in 1928 when the age was lowered to 21, the same age as male suffrage. This is an interesting case study as it relates to the development of democracy in the UK and indicates the depth of feeling held by many about this issue and their willingness to take direct action to pursue their cause.

Case study: equal pay for women

Before 1970, it was common for women in the UK, especially in the private sector, to be paid lower rates of pay than men, regardless of their skill levels.

In 1968, women sewing machinists at Ford's Dagenham factory went on strike demanding equal pay. This led to a number of other equal pay strikes and the start of a national campaign led by the trade unions. A massive equal pay demonstration took place in May 1969. The Equal Pay Act of 1970 permitted equal pay claims to be made by women in the public and private sector if their work was deemed the same, or broadly similar to, the work of their male equivalents.

Examiner tip

While the two examples here relate to campaigns in the past, be aware of case studies you could use that are more contemporary. When answering a question on this topic, can you remember the name of the group involved? Can you identify the cause? Did they achieve their aim? Why is/was their campaign important?

Websites

Women's battle for the vote:
http://news.bbc.co.uk/2/hi/uk_news/53819.stm
Did the Dagenham women's equal pay fight make a difference?
www.bbc.co.uk/news/magazine-11420445
The history of equal pay:
www.paywizard.co.uk/main/what-she-earns/equal-pay-history
www.unionhistory.info/equalpay/TeachersNotes.pdf

Examiner tip

In your chosen case study, use this framework when revising:

- Identify the group involved in the campaign.
- Identify the nature of their cause.
- What is the time frame for the events that took place?
- What were the reasons for the protest?
- What methods did the protesters use?
- To what extent did they achieve their aims?
- What was the impact of the change they brought about?
- Why do you believe this protest is an important citizenship case study?

Examiner tip

When revising, try to remember the key points identified as:

Who, **W**hat, **W**hen, **W**hy, and short-term, long-term **I**mpact.

Quick quiz online

Test yourself

Tested

1 Identify two basic freedoms of a citizen in the UK.
2 What is an 'active citizen'?
3 Identify one example of a campaign in regard to Human Rights in the UK.
4 What is meant by the term 'target group'?
5 How does a pressure group differ from a political party?

Exam practice

Unit 1, Short Course: Section A, Question 2

Read the source below and answer parts a), b) and c) which follow.

Source A

Pressure Group gets Council to Change Decision
In November last year the District Council decided by a small majority to close the Pannier Market, where weekly farmers' markets have been held for years. The council said that the building was no longer suitable and needed £500,000 spent on it to bring it up to current legal requirements. The stallholders and their customers set up a pressure group and over the last five months have campaigned to get the decision changed. They not only enlisted the help of the local MP and several of the MEPs, they also managed to get the support of a former local resident Paul Jones, who is now lead singer with the world famous boy band Trio. Paul asked his followers on Twitter to bombard the local council website and sign the online petition. Over 300,000 signed the online petition. At its March meeting the Council decided to overturn its earlier decision and seek funds to help restore the Pannier Market.

a) Identify three ways in which the stallholders sought to influence the council. *(3 marks)*

b) Outline three other methods the stallholders could have used to influence the council. *(3 marks)*

c) Why is the new e-media becoming an increasingly important campaigning tool? *(4 marks)*

Answers online ————————————————————————————— Online

U3 Recent UK-based case studies of campaigning

Revised

In recent years there has been a focus on campaigns that relate to broader issues often connected to the environment. These include issues such as climate change, road and rail building and airport extensions. The table below shows examples that could be included in case studies of campaigning.

Examiner tip

Make detailed revision notes about one successful and one unsuccessful campaign. Ensure that both are reasonably recent. Clearly identify why you think one was more successful than the other.

Jamie Oliver's School Dinners campaign	Started as a television programme on Channel 4 and eventually became a part of the Government's policy on healthy eating. www.jamieoliver.com/school-dinners
Hugh Fearnley-Whittingstall's Fish Fight campaign	Also used Channel 4 television as a platform for spearheading the campaign. www.fishfight.net
Save Our Forests campaign	In 2011, online petitions and marches led the Government to change its policy about selling off UK forests.
Student protests	In 2010, students and others protested about the Government's policy on university tuition fees and changes to the Educational Maintenance Allowance (EMA) for sixteen-to eighteen-year-olds. While both campaigns led to massive demonstrations and vast media coverage, neither achieved their aims.

U3 Factors in successful campaigning

Revised

The success or failure of any campaign can be due to a range of differing factors. Failure can be due to lack of public interest, an unpopular cause and/ or lack of media interest.

Successful campaigns and pressure groups have addressed some or all of the following key factors:

- whether the **nature of the cause** attracts public and/or media interest
- the **number of people** who support the cause or are members of the pressure group
- the **finance** available to the group to promote their cause
- the active support of the **media**
- the **methods used** to promote the cause
- the **status** of the group (is it an insider group working with those in power or is it an outsider group seeking to influence without any real contact with those in power?).

Use these factors when investigating any case study.

Some groups achieve their aims merely by their status and do not have to use any other methods. Many people say the Government cannot introduce changes in healthcare without the support of the medical profession, so bodies that represent doctors, such as the British Medical Association (BMA), can often achieve their aims without using campaigning methods due to their insider status. Some say that the National Farmers Union (NFU) has a similar influence over government policy relating to agriculture.

Examiner tip

Remember when answering a question to use the campaigns you have already identified as successes and failures and link their degree of success to the key factors listed opposite.

U3 Pressure groups and the media holding representatives to account

Revised

For most pressure group campaigns, the support of the media is important. Increasingly, the media themselves are taking campaigning stances, either by supporting existing campaigns or setting up their own. Through their activities, the media and pressure groups also maintain an oversight of the activities of our elected representatives.

In 2010, the *Daily Telegraph* published details of MPs' expenses, which led to a political scandal and a change in the way MPs' expenses are operated. It also led to several MPs and members of the House of Lords being arrested and put in jail for misuse of the expenses system for personal gain. This led to a large number of new MPs being elected in 2010.

Remember

Remember the term 'representatives' relates to both elected and non-elected individuals who hold power in the local community or nationally: local councillors, MPs, members of the House of Lords, Members of the European Parliament and members of the devolved assemblies.

In July 2000, the *News of the World* led a campaign regarding the naming of paedophiles in local areas. This resulted in a law being passed in Parliament that is known as Sarah's Law after Sarah Payne who was murdered by a convicted paedophile. The law permits parents to ask the police if someone who has access to their children has a record for child sex offences.

The examples of Channel 4's involvement in campaigning can be seen with Jamie Oliver's school meals and Hugh Fearnley-Whittingstall's fishing regulations mentioned on pages 19–20.

> **Websites**
> www.bbc.co.uk/news/
> uk-12952334

U3 Pressure group impact on public debate

Revised

The increasing use of the internet as a research tool has enabled individual citizens and pressure groups to research issues and campaigns. The internet also gives pressure groups a platform to promote their ideas, polices and/or research, which is not available to them through the traditional media. Also, more government information is now accessible to the public via the web and the Freedom of Information Act, 2005, which allows citizens and the media to ask questions and seek answers from government bodies.

Many pressure groups are called by government bodies, such as Select Committees, to give evidence as experts in a particular field. Within European Union decision-making processes, pressure groups and others that are recognised by the EU are formally involved in the debate and discussion regarding new proposals.

By using the media, pressure groups can often impact the political agenda. The whole debate on the non-issuing of plastic bags in shops started as a local campaign in Modbury, Devon, and has now become part of the Government's agenda with all the major supermarkets taking a stand in support of the campaign (see page 33 for more information on this campaign).

> **Examiner tip**
> When revising, investigate further one case study that has had an impact on public policy. Identify the issue. How did politicians respond? Why do you think they responded in that way?

> **Websites**
> www.channel4.com/
> lifestyle/green/green-
> people/hosking.html

Exam practice

Unit 3, Full Course: Section A, Question 1

Read the source below and answer parts a), b) and c) which follow.

Source A

> **A local group of protesters marched on the council offices to try to get the council to change its mind about closing a swimming pool.**

a) What type of action is the group taking? *(1 mark)*

b) Identify another form of action the protesters could take. *(2 marks)*

c) Which two groups do the protesters need to influence so that the decision is changed? *(2 marks)*

Answers online

Online

1.2 Who can make a difference?

Key terms

Charities – a voluntary group set up to help those in need. The term also has a legal status as charities registered with the Government receive some tax benefits.

Community – a defined group of citizens who normally reside in a given locality. Can be used to describe a school, part of a town or city.

Devolution – the transfer of power from a central body to a regional/local body.

Local government – different types of councils that provide services in a given local area.

Localism – the ability of people in a given local area to make decisions about policies affecting their local communities.

The media – means of communication. Mass media refers to communicating to a large number of people. The term 'new media' refers to e-media developments: the internet, social networking and blogging.

Tiers – a term used to describe different levels of government in the UK; each level has the same types of power/authority.

Trade unions – groups of workers who have joined together in order to protect their rights and to have an organisation to speak and negotiate on their behalf.

Voluntary groups – a term used to describe groups within local communities who give their time to help others.

Volunteering – the giving of a person's own time to help others without being paid.

U1 Community involvement

Revised

The two key ideas that are currently related to community involvement are 'localism' and 'The Big Society'. The first relates to central government allowing more local decision-making, and 'The Big Society' is a term that was first used by the Government in 2011 to describe the idea of a society where there are active citizens who volunteer and take an interest in their local communities.

Volunteering and local activism have always been seen as aspects of community life. Today people volunteer to work in charity shops, assist the Scouts or help with other groups. Even joining a political party or standing for election to your local council is a form of local activism/volunteering. Joining a local pressure group is also a form of local participation.

● Formal volunteering refers to people who volunteer with official groups, clubs or organisations.

● Informal volunteering refers to people who give unpaid help to other people, usually friends or neighbours.

● In England, 26 per cent of people participate in formal volunteering at least once a month.

● In England, 35 per cent of people participate in informal volunteering at least once a month.

Websites

www.direct.gov.uk/
en/YoungPeople/
Workandcareers/
Workexperienceand
volunteering/National
CitizenService/index.htm
www.volunteering.org.uk/
www.i-volunteer.org.uk/
www.volunteering.co.uk/

Examiner tip

To improve your answers to questions about volunteering, quote examples known to you, especially ones based in your local community. To research volunteering, look on your local council website for a list of local voluntary organisations.

Possible changes

In 2011, the Government introduced a National Citizenship Service for sixteen-year-olds, which encourages volunteering.

Examiner tip

Research some local case studies of volunteering and use them in any exam question about volunteering.

Remember

- 'Volunteering' is a very broad term covering a wide range of activities.
- Research indicates that a large number of people are involved in volunteering.
- Many aspects of life in your community would not exist if it were not for volunteers.
- Government policy relating to 'The Big Society' is reliant upon more people volunteering.

U1 Political power within the UK

Revised

The UK claims to be a democratic country in that all citizens over the age of eighteen are able to vote in elections, the Government can only serve for a certain time, we have a free media that can express a range of political opinions, the judiciary are separate from government and can, through the Supreme Court, express a view on legislation. While the UK doesn't have a written constitution like the USA, our constitution is made up of a variety of laws and conventions, which mean it is easier to amend. For example, the Human Rights Act of 1998 defined in law a number of citizens' rights.

Those we elect through the ballot box exercise political power. In the UK system of government, most power is held by central government. Central government is made up of the monarch, the House of Lords (currently unelected) and the House of Commons, made up of elected Members of Parliament (MPs) (see pages 34–5). Ultimate power resides with the House of Commons which passes laws that impact on all our lives. It is they who decide what other forms and tiers of government can exist in the UK. Parliament has the power to remove and replace any other form of government that exists in the UK.

Traditionally, power was divided between central government and local government. Local government is made up of elected councillors, and some areas now also have elected mayors. In the UK, the terms central and local have traditionally been used to describe the way in which government operates. Real power was held by central government and local government carried out locally the services that central government decided. Most of the funds for local government are provided by central government. Local government members, called councillors, are elected for periods of either three or four years and make many decisions about the local community, from roads to rubbish collection to planning permissions to public health issues. Councils raise the money they require beyond their government grant mainly from the Council Tax – a tax on property. Most local councillors stand using a political label and most councils are either controlled by one political party or by a coalition of parties. In some areas of the country there are still a number of councillors who stand as Independents, free of any political control.

Websites

www.parliament.uk/about/how/role/parliament-government/
www.localgov.co.uk/index.cfm
www.niassembly.gov.uk/
www.scottish.parliament.uk
www.london.gov.uk
www.wales.gov.uk

Remember

- Political power in the UK resides with Parliament, especially with the elected House of Commons.
- All other forms of government only exist because they were established by Parliament. Parliament has the power to abolish any other tier of government in the UK.
- Parliament is accountable for its actions to the citizens of the UK at general elections.

Since 1997, central government has decided that forms of devolved government should exist in Scotland, Wales and London, and devolved power would be returned to Northern Ireland. Devolved power had existed in Northern Ireland since 1921 but had been withdrawn in 1972 (due to the conflict in Northern Ireland) when direct rule (rule by the UK Government) was introduced.

Currently we have a tiered local government system in the UK involving:

Parish, District, County and Unitary councils – which each deliver a different range of local services.

Regional or devolved national government in London, Wales, Scotland and Northern Ireland.

Central government – based upon Parliament in London.

Beyond central government is the European Union (EU), which is also able to pass laws and regulations that impact on people's lives in the UK.

Examiner tip

To help you revise, design a simple table divided into levels, starting with the smallest type of council in your area. Find out its name and title and the services it provides by researching these on the internet. Move up the levels until you come to the UK's central government.

Another key way to understand the importance of each tier of government is to look at the size of their budgets – how much do they each spend each year?

Examiner tip

When revising, to help you understand the nature of political power in the UK, start with your own local community.

- Who are your local councillors?
- Who is your constituency Member of Parliament?
- Who represents your area in the European Parliament?

All these people have websites through which they can be contacted and asked about the work they do for your local community.

U1 The influence of the media in influencing or reflecting public opinion

Revised

Many people are concerned about the power and influence of the media in setting the political agenda.

- Some people think the media are too influential and that politicians often merely follow the issues published in the press because they want newspapers to support them at the next election.

- Other people say that the media only reflects what the public is thinking and that it is the politicians who are out of touch with public opinion.

- Other people argue that the power of the media to influence people's views is overestimated because in the UK, television – which is currently the major way most citizens gain their information – is regulated regarding ownership and has to be impartial in regard to politics.

Examiner tip

Research several different types of media, both traditional and e-media. To understand the influence of the press/TV/e-media, carry out some web research on one day and compare which stories hit the headlines and how they are reported. For political stories, look at what comments/views are expressed by the authors of the stories.

Newspapers often set a broad political agenda in regard to a government or the opposition by portraying them as being in control or out of control and as weak, strong or divided. Over a period of time they try to establish this agenda with their readers.

The table below shows newspaper support at the 2010 General Election. Most local daily and weekly papers do not take a political stand but will often support local causes or campaigns.

Labour	Liberal Democrats	Conservatives
The Daily Mirror *Sunday Mirror*	*The Guardian* *The Independent* *The Observer*	*The Telegraph* *The Sun* *The Daily Express* *The Daily Mail* *The Times*

If it were not for the *Telegraph* the full extent of the MPs' expenses scandal would not have been exposed. Similarly, the *Guardian* newspaper campaigned over a long period about newspaper phone hacking and the *News of the World* campaigned for Sarah's Law.

Increasingly, the power of the internet to influence views is distracting from the power of the traditional media. The internet is immediate and has no real form of censorship.

Possible changes

The 2011 public inquiry into the media after the phone hacking scandal will have produced a lot of material about the power and influence of the media.

Remember

- Remember that the term 'the media' embraces a range of different formats, not just newspapers.
- Television in the UK is regulated and has to be politically impartial.
- New media, or e-media, is becoming increasingly important. It is not controlled and is citizen-led.
- Many newspapers have led successful campaigns to bring about change.
- Most national newspapers are linked to political parties when elections are held. This can lead to close relations between the owners/editors of newspapers and politicians.

Test yourself

Tested ☐

1 What do we mean by the term 'mass media'?
2 How does the political stand taken by newspapers differ from that taken by television in the UK?

Quick quiz online

Websites

United Kingdom country profile:
http://news.bbc.co.uk/1/hi/world/europe/country_profiles/1038758.stm

Examiner tip

Remember that the exam practice question below is asked in the context of 'Who can make a difference?' so the word 'councillor' is being used in the context of the specification – for example, someone elected to a local authority/council. The trigger word is 'role', which often causes candidates problems. Think of it as asking what they do.

Exam practice

Unit 1, Short Course: Section A, Question 1

a) What is the role of a councillor? *(1 mark)*

Answers online ──────── Online ☐

U3 Trade unions

- Trade unions are groups of workers that have joined together in order to protect their rights and to have an organization to speak and negotiate on their behalf.

- Most trade unions in the UK date from the end of the nineteenth century or the early part of the twentieth century.

- In recent years the membership of unions has declined and many have merged to form larger unions.

- The unions have more members in the public sector than the private sector. In the UK, most trade unions belong to the Trades Union Congress.

- The trade unions formally established the Labour Party in 1900. Many unions have political funds and donate money to support the Labour Party. The unions are the Labour Party's largest source of income.

- For many years the trade unions were a major political force in the UK, but since 1979 their political influence has been in decline.

- Laws passed by Parliament govern most trade union activity.

- In 2009, just over 7 million workers belonged to trade unions.

Examiner tip

Research at least two different trade unions. Remember their names or initials. How many members do they have? What jobs do their members undertake? What campaigns are they currently undertaking?

Laws regulate the action unions can take in support of their members – for example, if they wish to strike the members must vote for the action in a secret ballot. One group of workers cannot take strike action to support another group of workers already on strike. This is called secondary action and was outlawed by the Employment Act of 1990.

Websites

www.tuc.org.uk

People join trade unions for a variety of reasons. Many people join a union for protection and to safeguard their rights, and to have someone to turn to and speak on their behalf. Union membership can also give members social and financial benefits. On joining a union, a member has to pay a regular subscription. At some places of work, the employer has agreed that the workforce can only join one union, this is called a Single Union Agreement, and this ensures that the employer has only one union with which to negotiate.

U3 The impact of collective action

The impact of collective action can be both beneficial and negative. Collective action can involve:

- **strikes**–where workers withdraw their labour because of a grievance

- **walkouts**–where workers stop work and leave the workplace in order to protest

- **working to rule**–where workers do only what they are required to do by the rules of the workplace or their contract.

Sometimes workers achieve their desired aims and return to work, but sometimes action can be so damaging to the employer that they close the place of employment. Different strikes can have a different impact on local communities. If teachers went on strike in a local area, the impact would be felt by parents who may have to stay at home to look after children; this

Examiner tip

Research a current strike or industrial action by a trade union.

- What is the issue?

- How has the employer reacted?

- Have any third parties tried to intervene to resolve the situation?

- How was the issue resolved?

would then impact upon their employers. If the action was in a community where the employer was the major employer, a strike could have a devastating impact. If many thousands were on strike, it would affect many businesses in the community as strikers have less money to spend and the employer doesn't need the services of other businesses in the community. In the 1980s, following industrial action, the closure of many coalmines destroyed the viability of many communities.

U3 The impact of government on the lives of citizens

Revised

The Government impacts hugely on the lives of its citizens. One way of studying this issue is to look at yourself as an individual from birth until death and identify the ways in which government impacts upon your life. The following list gives you a starting point for your revision.

Examiner tip

The focus of this element of the course is the impact upon the citizen, so answer any question by focusing on this aspect. Remember you can use case studies and base your response on your experiences and those from your local community.

Birth: A woman giving birth in a hospital uses government-funded health services.

↓

Childhood: Benefits are paid by government to families on Child Benefit. Some child care/nursery provision is government-funded.

↓

School age: Children may attend school until the age of seventeen. The schools are government-funded.

↓

Working age: A family on a low income or in need of housing is supported by the government. For those unable to find work there is a government benefit system to provide support.

↓

Pension age: Government makes provision for those in old age, including pension provision.

You can also look at the broader services provided by government – for example, protection of its citizens – from the provision of the armed forces to the justice system and policing. Government also passes laws, which impact on our lives. You could study this topic through age-related laws (see page 70). Government also impacts on our lives by its taxation and revenue-raising policies, which are needed to pay for the services it provides – for example, VAT, income tax, National Insurance.

Some people would argue that the Government is too heavily involved in our lives while others would say that it needs to do more regarding equality and discrimination. You could prepare for the exam by looking at potential questions about different views on this.

U3 The issue of non-participation within communities

Revised

Society can only function fully if its citizens participate and have a sense of belonging and ownership. Apathy exists when people are not interested, do not care about what happens and do not participate, especially in the democratic process. Democracy is based upon the idea of citizens' involvement. If all citizens do not become involved, only those who do participate exercise power and influence.

In the UK, the lowest turnout in elections is among 18- to 24-year-olds and the highest is among the over-65-year-olds. If you were a politician seeking election, which group would you aim your policies at if you wished to get elected – those who vote or those who don't?

The major political parties in the UK each have a declining membership – people are increasingly joining pressure groups or single-issue groups rather than political parties.

- In the 2001 General Election only 59 per cent of electors voted.

- In the 2010 General Election the voter turnout was below 50 per cent in some constituencies. In Leeds Central the turnout was 46 per cent.

Non-participation can lead to alienation from society and lead to anti-social behaviour.

Examiner tip

To revise this part of the course, try to find examples or case studies of non-participation from your own community to use in your exam responses. These may include low turnout in elections or the age profile of community groups and councillors. Consider how people can be encouraged to participate.

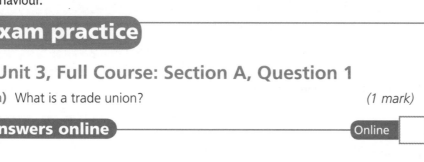

Exam practice

Unit 3, Full Course: Section A, Question 1

a) What is a trade union? *(1 mark)*

Answers online ———————————————— Online

1.3 How and why are Citizenship issues relevant in the workplace?

Key terms

Employers – individuals or organisations that employ others to work on their behalf.

Employment tribunal – official body established in law to hear and resolve issues relating to work and employment. Their decisions are binding and enforceable.

Equal opportunities – allowing all people equality of access to opportunities throughout their lives. Often associated with government legislation to promote equality.

Health and safety – matters that relate to the health and safety of employees, customers and visitors at any place of work. These issues are legally enforceable and are overseen by the Health and Safety Executive (HSE).

NEETs – young people who after leaving school are not in work or training. Stands for 'Not in Education, Employment or Training'.

Rights – an authority to carry out a course of action, e.g. a policeman has the right to arrest a person suspected of committing a crime.

Responsibilities – as well as having rights as a citizen, states expect citizens to perform certain duties. For example, in time of war a nation may conscript citizens into the armed forces.

Self-employed – someone who does not have an employer but works for his or her self.

Sustainability – a policy whereby what is produced or made does as little damage to raw materials or resources as possible by encouraging the replacement of the materials used, e.g. in forestry for every tree cut down another is planted.

Trade unions – groups of workers that join together to support and negotiate on behalf of their members.

Unemployed – a person without work, normally registered with a Job Centre and claiming state benefit.

U1 Rights and responsibilities in the workplace
 Revised

If an employee thinks they have been badly treated by their employer they can bring a case before an Employment Tribunal which can make a legally binding decision. Most workers are represented by their union at tribunal hearings. Most employers and trade unions try to arrive at an agreement prior to a hearing as the hearings are public events and the proceedings can be published.

Health and safety issues can have an impact upon employees, employers and customers. Prior to the examination ensure you are aware of at least two different types of health and safety issues.

What is discrimination?

Equal opportunities legislation aims to prevent people being treated unfairly so that people are only employed, paid, trained and promoted based on their qualifications, skills, abilities and how they do their job.

Examples of discrimination in the workplace could include a female employee being paid less than a male colleague for doing the same job, or an ethnic minority employee being refused the training opportunities offered to white colleagues.

Examiner tip

When revising, in relation to workers' rights, focus on two or three rights and try to flesh out a case study. For example, the minimum wage – ensure you know the current rate and research the types of business that pay at that rate. Is the rate set too high or low?

Websites

The following website provides a number of case studies regarding health and safety issues:
www.hse.gov.uk/resources/casestudies.htm.

Employee rights	Employee responsibilities	Employer rights	Employer responsibilities
To receive a written statement detailing your employment requirements	To report concerns about safety	To expect employees to work as per their agreed contracts	To provide clear policies in regard to employees' rights
To be paid the National Minimum Wage	To abide by the terms of your contract	To expect reasonable behaviour by the workforce by using the agreed structures for raising issues	To work within all health and safety regulations
To have protection from unlawful deductions from wages	To follow health and safety regulations	To have the ability to be able to negotiate with trade unions regarding changing work practices	To pay wages as negotiated and to take account of the national minimum wage
To have paid holiday	To work the hours required by your contract	Employees to work at the agreed time and take only the agreed breaks during the working day	To provide holiday entitlement and wages
To have limits on your working hours	To follow the employees' absence policy		To negotiate with trade unions in regard to changes in regard to conditions of employment
To have the ability to join a trade union	To follow reasonable instructions regarding your work		To work with the law in regard to all employment practices
To be safe in the workplace	To be a part of the work appraisal processes		
To have compassionate leave as a result of personal circumstances, for example death of a relative	To work within the law as it impacts upon your employment		

An employer is not allowed to discriminate against a person because of their:

- gender
- marriage or civil partnership
- gender reassignment
- pregnancy or maternity leave
- sexual orientation
- disability
- race
- colour
- ethnic background
- nationality
- religion or belief
- age.

Examiner tip

Work your revision around a case study. Where possible, use real-life examples. Look at cases that are currently before industrial tribunals, which you can find by searching news websites.

An employer must treat employees who work part-time or who are on fixed-term contracts as they do full-time employees.

Types of discrimination

Direct discrimination happens when an employer treats an employee less favourably than someone else for one of the reasons shown above. For example, it would be direct discrimination if a driving job were only open to male applicants.

Indirect discrimination is when a working condition or rule disadvantages one group of people more than another. For example, saying that applicants for a job must be clean-shaven puts members of some religious groups at a disadvantage.

Harassment means offensive or intimidating behaviour – sexist language or racial abuse that aims to humiliate, undermine or injure its target or has that effect – for example, giving someone an offensive nickname. You have the right not to be harassed or made fun of at work or in a work-related setting.

Victimisation means treating somebody less favourably than someone else because they tried to make, or made, a complaint about discrimination – for example, preventing them from going on a course or taking unfair disciplinary action against them.

Consumer rights

As consumers of goods and services, we have certain statutory rights. When you buy goods they should be:

- **of satisfactory quality** – last for the time you would expect them to and be free of any defects

- **fit for purpose** – fit for the use described and any specific use you discussed with the seller

- **as described** – match the description on the packaging or what the seller told you.

If an item does not meet any of these rights, it is faulty and you will usually have the right to a:

- repair
- replacement
- refund.

Various pieces of legislation in the UK provide the legal framework for consumer protection:

The Sale of Goods Act, 1979 states that goods must be as described in any literature or advertisement, of satisfactory quality and fit for the purpose; this means if you requested a printer that works with a computer it must work with that computer.

The Sale of Goods and Services Act 1982 aims to protect consumers against bad workmanship or the poor provision of services – for example if a builder fails to keep to an agreement you made with them. It also applies to everyday situations – such as going to the hairdressers or the dry cleaners – where you have no written contract or agreement.

If you as a consumer feel you have not been treated correctly, you can contact your local Trading Standards Officers who are employed by local councils. The role of a trading standards officer (TSO) is to act on behalf of consumers and businesses to advise on and enforce laws that govern the way goods and services are bought, sold or hired. They must ensure compliance with legislation such as the Consumer Protection from Unfair Trading Regulations 2008, the Consumer Protection Act and the Weights and Measures Act.

In regard to broader trading issues the Government established the Office of Fair Trading (OFT) which carries out investigations into company practices on behalf of the public. Examples include a report warning people to steer clear of scam loan companies that take up-front fees but fail to provide credit or offer clearly unsuitable credit alternatives, and urging gyms to check their contract terms to make sure they are lawful after the High Court ordered a gym management company not to use certain unfair terms. The public are able to contact the OFT and if sufficient complaints are made it can trigger an inquiry.

As an EU member, consumer protection directives from the EU apply to the UK.

Examiner tip

Ensure when you revise that you have knowledge of some recent case studies relating to consumer rights. These can be researched from news websites, or you may wish to contact your local Trading Standards officials based at your local council offices, who are responsible for investigating complaints and carrying out investigations.

Websites

www.britishlaw.org.uk/cit_cons.html
www.direct.gov.uk
www.adviceguide.org.uk

Possible changes

New regulations are increasingly introduced after an issue emerges – for example, protection for workers' pensions when a firm goes bankrupt or increasing the amount of savings that are protected if a financial institution fails.

Examiner tip

Remember that all the question parts in Question 1 are to be answered. Some may appear more difficult than others, but they should not require longer answers.

Exam practice

Unit 1, Short Course: Section A, Question 1

a) Identify one consumer right. *(1 mark)*

b) Why can't an employer advertise for men only to apply for employment? *(1 mark)*

Answers online Online ☐

Examiner tip

The trigger word 'identify' in exam practice question a) means just outline one right. Support it with an example, even though it is not asked for, as this will show the examiner that you understand the term.

U3 The economy and community cohesion   Revised ☐

- Many local communities rely upon the strength of particular local businesses to provide work and employment for local people.

- Where local communities are too dependent upon one type of employment they are at risk if that business goes into decline. The closure of most of the coal-mining industry at the end of the last century left many towns and communities devastated. This decline can lead to a breakdown in community cohesion between those who are employed and those who are not.

- A strong economy is important for a cohesive society. If a country has an expanding economy it tends to have rising employment and falling unemployment. The level of taxation available to government increases and that allows the government to provide more benefits and services for its citizens. This sense of economic well being lowers tensions within society – for example, such periods of time normally have lower levels of crime.

- A weak economy leads to unemployment and lower taxation for the government, and this in turn can lead to cuts in government support and help.

- As the nature of a developing economy changes, so does its impact upon its citizens. Large-scale manufacturing carried out by low-paid workers is now largely done overseas. The UK economy now designs and provides services – for example, finance to support cheaper production overseas.

Examiner tip

The economy is a vast subject, so when revising, focus on case studies of local communities or types of industry in order to study the impact of change. For example, you could examine the changing pattern of holidaying – how has that impacted upon traditional holiday areas in the UK? Or, where there were major employers, like shipbuilding or iron and steel producers, what is happening in those communities now those industries have gone?

This is done to enable the goods produced to be sold at a competitive price in overseas markets.

● Where there is growth in manufacturing it is in high-cost, high-value goods such as motor vehicles.

U3 Case studies: sustainable practices

Revised

When you go shopping in supermarkets today, you are increasingly asked whether you are using your own bags or wish to purchase a reusable bag instead of using a use-once-and-throw-away plastic bag. At the 2010 General Election, the political parties mentioned the use of plastic bags in their manifestoes.

Case study: banning the use of plastic bags

● In April 2007, 43 shops in Modbury, a small town in Devon, decided to ban the use of plastic bags for six months and encourage shoppers to use cotton reusable bags. The trial was so successful that the plastic bag ban was made permanent. The campaign was started by Rebecca Hoskin, a wildlife photographer, who was appalled by the amount of bags she saw when filming in the sea.

● The campaign gained widespread support and by 2009 the use of plastic bags had been reduced by half.

● The prime minister at the time, Gordon Brown, ordered every government department to stop buying branded plastic bags.

● Seven major supermarket chains – ASDA, the Co-operative, Marks & Spencer, Sainsbury's, Somerfield, Tesco and Waitrose – agreed a new target to cut the number of single-use bags handed out by half.

Exam practice

Unit 3, Full Course: Section A, Question 1

Read the source below and answer questions a) to c).

Source A

> The number of strikes in the UK has decreased over recent years. Many people put this down to changes in the law, which ensure ballots are held before a strike can take place.

a) What is a strike? *(1 mark)*

b) Identify two other actions a union can take to support workers other than call for a strike. *(2 marks)*

c) Explain why there are fewer strikes today than 30 years ago. *(2 marks)*

Answers online ———————————————————— Online

Examiner tip

This is a case where an individual, then a community, tried to make a difference and persuaded others, so that what started in one small town is now an international campaign. Carry out some research into what is happening in your local community. Also look at major national businesses to see what they are doing. Car manufacturers are now required to use more recycled materials and dispose of old cars. Many businesses are developing micro power plants where spare electricity is sold to the national grid.

Examiner tip

The source in the exam practice question provides some background, but do not always expect to find the answers in the source.

2.1 What are the roles of Parliament and Government?

Key terms

Devolution – a process where power and authority are shared between different bodies. In the UK, the central government agreed to share power and authority with elected bodies in Scotland, Wales and Northern Ireland. Their national Assemblies and Parliaments are sometimes referred to as 'devolved bodies'.

Government – the individuals who run the state. In the UK we refer to central government, which is made up of the political party or parties that won the general election. The prime minister leads the government and appoints other ministers.

Parliament – currently understood as the institution of government in the UK where those elected and appointed meet to pass laws. It comprises three parts: the House of Commons, the House of Lords and the monarch.

Political literacy – the ability to participate in the political process, developed through political knowledge and understanding.

U1 What is Parliament? Its composition and main roles

Revised

Parliament and its composition

Parliament comprises three parts: the House of Commons, the House of Lords and the monarch.

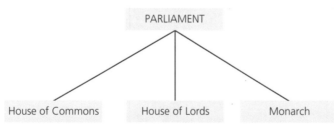

The House of Commons is made up of 646 Members of Parliament (MPs) who are elected by the people at a general election. Governments are formed after the outcome of a general election, decided by which party or parties normally have a majority of MPs.

The House of Lords is currently made up of appointed Life Peers (Lords), who are appointed for life and whose title dies with them, and a few remaining Hereditary Peers whose families have held titles for generations.

The monarch is the third element of our parliamentary system. He/she has given most of his/her powers to the Prime Minister and other ministers, but still has to sign all laws after they have been passed by Parliament, and must agree if the Prime Minister wishes to call a general election.

Up to 2010, general elections were called by the Prime Minister, although there has to be an election within five years of the last election. In 2011, the government proposed a law that would fix the dates of general elections (Fixed-term Parliaments).

At a general election every constituency (seat) elects one Member of Parliament, every voter has one vote and the winner is the candidate with the most votes. Elections are traditionally held on a Thursday and the polling stations where people vote are open from 8a.m.–10p.m. The votes are counted after 10p.m., the overall result of the general election is normally known during the middle of the night, but some results are not known until later on the Friday.

The party that has a majority of the seats in Parliament (MPs) forms the government. The monarch officially asks the leader of that party to form a government. At the 2010 General Election, no party gained a majority of the seats so a coalition government was formed when the Conservative and Liberal Democrats agreed to work together in government.

Role of Parliament

MPs are elected to represent the electorate for a given area (a constituency) with approximately 72,000 electors. They represent their local area and deal with any issues on behalf of their constituents. They cannot deal with problems raised by people outside of their constituency.

The major function of Parliament is to pass laws (legislation). There are only three major types of laws:

● those proposed by the Government

● those proposed by individual MPs

● private bills on behalf of organisations (for example, local government).

Government Bills (proposals that become law) account for most of the laws passed.

Parliament also holds government to account for its actions. The Government, opposition parties or MPs can call for emergency statements or debates on topical issues. Committees of MPs and Lords scrutinise proposed legislation in detail.

Possible changes

● The number of MPs elected to the House of Commons is being reduced. Look out for debate and discussion about the number of MPs for your local area.

● The House of Lords is currently subject to proposals for its reform. Some people wish to see an all or partially elected House of Lords.

● In 2011, the Government passed a law for fixed-term Parliaments – an election every five years on a known date.

● In 2011 it is being proposed that in future the monarchy will be handed down through the eldest child rather than the eldest boy.

Remember, a lot of changes happen in Parliament, so check websites such as www.bbc.co.uk/news/politics/ prior to the exam to see if any further changes have been made.

Remember

The specification refers to 'roles' – this means what it does and what its function is.

● The role of Parliament: to represent the views of the people through elected MPs; holds governments to account. This is achieved by holding debates and votes in the House of Commons, votes and discussions in committees; select committee shadow government departments and call ministers to account, other committees study proposed legislation and can suggest amendments (changes).

● The role of government: to pass laws and debate issues. Governments can be defeated in votes and sometimes this means that they have to resign and a new election held – for example, this happened in 1979.

Websites

www.direct.gov.uk
www.parliament.uk
www.bbc.co.uk/news/politics/

Examiner tip

When revising, try to recall one major law that has been passed recently. Each year look out for the Budget, which is the major finance Bill for the year. Normally in the autumn the Queen gives the Queen's Speech about what laws the government are proposing for the following year. The speech is actually written by the government.

U1 How laws are made by Parliament

All types of proposals for laws go through the same stages.

The Green Paper
Often the Government will publish a 'Green Paper', which is a discussion document about a possible new law, and invite MPs and others to comment upon its suggestions. It is called Green because the cover is green.

The First Reading
The Government then publishes a 'White Paper', which is a proposal for a new law. This becomes a Bill (draft law) and is formerly announced (First Reading) in the House of Commons. No debate takes place at this time.

The Second Reading
This stage involves a debate upon the principle of the proposed legislation and a vote takes place at the end of the debate.

The Committee Stage
This stage comes next, where a group of MPs from all parties discuss the Bill in detail, line by line, and vote on amendments.

The Report Stage
The work of the committee is discussed and voted upon in the House of Commons.

The Third Reading (or Final Stage)
The amended legislation is voted upon and the legislation is then sent to the House of Lords where all the same stages from First Reading to Third Reading are gone through. If the Lords make amendments, the Bill returns to the House of Commons where further votes take place until the Bill is accepted.

The Royal Assent
The legislation then receives Royal Assent – it is agreed and signed by the monarch – and then becomes Law.

Remember
Remember the order of key events. Being able to recall a recent law that has come into force is very helpful. You don't need to know its full title, just what it is about.

Private Members' Bills

Private Members' Bills are laws proposed by individual MPs who are not government ministers. The names of MPs applying for a Bill are put into a ballot and those whose names are pulled out first, second or third stand the best chance of getting a Bill through Parliament. Those MPs whose names are pulled out earliest are often approached by charities and organisations to promote ideas they have for legislation. Private Members' Bills cannot involve raising taxation. They are often about social issues – for example, abortion, divorce or homosexuality – where there are no party divisions. Very few become law each year.

> **Remember**
> * Stage, Report Stage and Third Reading; then to the House of Lords, where amendments are considered, and finally becomes law on receiving the Royal Assent. Some Bills start in the Lords.
> * Public Bills = proposed by the Government.
> * Private Members' Bills = proposed by individual MPs.
> * Private Bills = sponsored by organisations such as local councils (byelaws).

U1 What are the roles of political parties, government and opposition, and the Cabinet?

Revised

A **political party** is a group of people who share the same political ideas (ideology) and work together to achieve power at a local and national level. Parties can be national or regional – for example, the Labour Party is national, and the Scottish Nationalist Party (Scotland) and the Ulster Unionist Party (Northern Ireland) are regional.

The Government is the party or parties that are in power and run the government.

The opposition is all those parties who are not in government – who are 'in opposition' to the Government. The largest opposition party is given the title 'Her Majesty's Official Opposition' and sits opposite the Government in the House of Commons. Its leader and Chief Whip are paid the same salaries as government ministers.

The Cabinet is senior members of the Government who hold ministerial jobs.

* The law limits the number of ministers in the Cabinet. If a prime minister wants more ministers, they have to be unpaid. Ministers receive more pay than MPs.

* The most senior ministers are the Foreign Secretary, the Chancellor of the Exchequer and the Home Secretary.

* The Cabinet meets regularly at 10 Downing Street to discuss the business of government.

* The Prime Minister chairs meetings of the Cabinet and sets Cabinet committees to debate and discuss issues of government policy. Many claim that in the UK we have a 'Cabinet Government', which means that a prime minister has to work with his Cabinet to survive. But many now say that prime ministers are becoming more powerful and Cabinets less powerful.

* The Prime Minister decides who is in the Cabinet and can sack them at any time.

> **Examiner tip**
> Try to remember the names of the major UK political parties: the Conservatives, the Labour Party and the Liberal Democrats.

Possible changes

The Cabinet often changes – ministers can be promoted or sacked – so prior to the exam check the current composition of the Cabinet and their titles. Be aware that sometime the names of ministries can change – for example, education has been DfES, DES and DfE.

Websites

www.number10.gov.uk
www.cabinetoffice.gov.uk
www.labour.org.uk
www.conservativeparty.org.uk
www.libdems.org.uk
www.snp.org.uk
www.plaidcymru.org
www.mydup.com
www.sinnfein.ie

Remember

Remember the term 'roles' relates to what people do and their power – for example, the prime minister is the leader of the government and has the power to appoint his Cabinet, decide when a general election is held, decide the government's agenda and make numerous appointments, as well as being leader of his political party.

Test yourself

Tested ☐

1 Which party or parties currently form the Government of the UK?
2 Can you name any two political parties that only stand for election in one part of the UK?
3 What is the difference between a Public Bill and a Private Members' Bill?
4 What happens at the Committee Stage?
5 Identify the three key Cabinet posts, after the Prime Minister.

Quick quiz online

Exam practice

Unit 1 Short Course: Section B, Question 3

Read the source below and answer parts a), b) and c) which follow.

Source A

Scotland to leave the UK
Leading pollsters are predicting that in the forthcoming referendum on Scottish independence, 53 per cent will vote for full independence for Scotland. It is estimated that only 40 per cent of voters will turn out to vote. The UK Prime Minister has stated that he is opposed to Scotland withdrawing from the Union, as have the leaders of all the major UK parties. The leader of the Scottish Parliament has said that what is important is the will of the people of Scotland and the UK Parliament should not try to block Scottish independence.

a) What do you understand by the term 'the Union'?   (2 marks)

b) Briefly outline the case a UK prime minister could make to the people of Scotland to vote 'no' in the referendum.   (6 marks)

c) What are the advantages for Scotland if it gained full independence?   (12 marks)

Answers online   Online ☐

U3 Recent changes to the operation of democracy in the UK

Revised

Devolution

Following referendums in Scotland (1997), Wales (1997) and Northern Ireland (1998), which resulted in a vote for devolved powers, assemblies and parliaments were established in these UK countries. The bodies came into existence in 1999. Both Wales and Northern Ireland have assemblies, which have slightly fewer powers than the Parliament established in Scotland. All three hold elections using a proportional system. In the case of Northern Ireland, a coalition government must be formed based upon parties representing both communities in Northern Ireland (the Ulster Unionists and the Nationalist/Republican community).

Recent changes

The Government is currently considering changes to the House of Lords and the number of MPs in the House of Commons. All constitutional reforms are currently the responsibility of the Deputy Prime Minister.

Examiner tip

When revising, look at the websites of the devolved bodies (see Websites) to understand their current composition and powers.

Websites

www.scottish.parliament.uk
www.niassembly.gov.uk
www.wales.gov.uk
Look at this website to see current proposals for constitutional changes:
www.dpm.cabinetoffice.gov.uk

U3 How are citizens' lives affected by the way in which governments and politicians exercise power at a national level?

Revised

The specification details the following aspects of what can be a very broad topic: economic management, taxation and public services. You need to be aware in broad terms of how the UK public finances operate, i.e. the level of public spending, what major services cost to run and where the money is raised.

The table below indicates UK Government spending and income for 2011/12:

UK Government Spending 2011/12	UK Government Income 2011/12
Debt interest – £50 billion Public order and safety – £33 billion Housing and Environment £24 billion Industry, agriculture and employment – £20 billion Defence – £40 billion Education – £89 billion Transport – £23 billion Social protection – £200 billion Personal social services – £32 billion Health – £126 billion Other – £74 billion	Council tax – £26 billion Business rates – £25 billion VAT – £100 billion Corporation tax – £48 billion Income Tax – £158 billion National Insurance – £101 billion Excise duties – £46 billion Other – £85 billion

The table includes Council Tax, which is collected by local councils. The ways in which governments decide to raise and spend public money can have a large impact upon citizens. Examples include raising university tuition fees, raising the rate of VAT to 20 per cent (Value Added Tax – a payment added to the cost of most goods that people buy).

Examiner tip

You only need to have an idea of the overall size of the budget, main spenders and main sources of revenue when answering exam questions.

Websites

For current details of public spending and taxation see www.hm-treasury.gov.uk.

2.1 What are the roles of Parliament and Government?

Spending less money on certain services can impact directly upon citizens. If certain benefits are cut, some people have less income. When more money is spent, the Government also has to consider whether to raise taxes or increase the public debt (borrowing money to pay back later).

In regards to economic management, the UK economy generally works as a free market capitalist system based upon private ownership. In most economies in the world, some services are provided by government and some by private firms.

- In a **controlled economy** all aspects are controlled by the Government – this type of economy was associated with the former Communist countries like the USSR.

- **Private/Free enterprise** or **Market economies** rely upon private ownership of the means of production and services: people either own their own businesses or people can invest in businesses by buying shares and receiving dividends (part of the profits). The USA operates as a free enterprise economy. The phrase also relates to limited government intervention in the workings of the economy.

- Where economies have both large private and publicly owned sectors in the economy they are called **mixed economies**.

The amount of ownership in the hands of the state in the UK has declined rapidly since 1979 under all parties in government. In 2011, a major political debate concerned the extent to which the private sector of business should be involved in running remaining state-provided services – for example, the NHS and education. There was also a debate in the UK about the level of provision of public services and the level of taxation.

U3 UK democracy compared with other forms of government, including one European or wider world, and one non-democratic system

Revised

A **democracy** is a political system of government in which power resides with the people, governments are fairly elected and subject to regular elections, the election system is secret and open to all. A free press exists to report on government and that government is also accountable to the legal system and separate from it. Government is based upon constitutional principles in a formal constitutional document or in laws. The country respects the human rights of its citizens.

Other types of government include:

- **monarchy** – government by a family based upon hereditary principles

- **oligarchy** – government by an elite few, normally self-appointed

- **dictatorship/totalitarianism** – rule by an individual or group with no democratic aspects to the state; total control by one person or group

- **one party/communist** – government by one party; choice limited to officially approved candidates

- **anarchy** – a state without any form of government/control

- **theocracy** – a state based upon religious belief.

Examiner tip

The questions asked will be general and you will be expected to use the countries you have studied as examples, where suitable.

Websites

Human Rights Watch at www.hrw.org provides up-to-date information regarding human rights abuse across the world. You can use this site to monitor any countries you choose to study.

Once you are clear about the definitions on page 40, carry out some research into countries that fit the profile. China, Cuba and Vietnam would count as one-party states. Use the definition above to confirm if they have any elements of what we in the UK think should be in a democracy. With the end of the Cold War, most countries within Europe would claim to be democratic. It is one of the conditions for a country that wishes to join either NATO or the EU.

Exam practice

Unit 3, Full Course: Section A, Question 2

Read the source below and answer questions a) to c).

Source A

2010 General Election Result	
Conservatives	307 MPs
Labour	258 MPs
Liberal Democrats	57 MPs
Others	28 MPs

a) Identify one political party that is included within the 28 other MPs? *(1 mark)*

b) Who won the General Election of 2010? *(2 marks)*

c) Outline briefly **one** role of an MP at Westminster. *(2 marks)*

Answers online _____ Online

2.2 How can citizens participate in democratic processes, particularly elections and voting?

Key terms

Elections (electoral process) – a system whereby citizens within a country are able to vote and the outcome of the elections gives those elected the authority to govern. Elections are held at regular intervals. Currently UK general elections are held on fixed dates.

Democracy – a society where citizens, through an open and fair electoral system, are able to vote in regular elections, where a range of different political ideas are allowed, where governments are accountable and there is a respect for human rights and a 'free press' – a press not restricted or controlled by the Government.

Lobbying – a general term about making your views known to those whose opinions you wish to influence. The specific term relates to citizens approaching their Member of Parliament to raise an issue. This is done in the Lobby of the House of Commons.

Voting systems – the method of voting used in an election. In the UK a range of differing voting systems are used. One key element of all voting systems in the UK is that the decision made by each voter is secret.

U1 How fair and effective are existing voting systems in the UK?

Revised

UK voting systems

In the UK, every citizen over the age of eighteen is entitled to vote. In order to vote, your name must appear on the Register of Electors. It is the citizen's responsibility to check that their name is on the list. When an election of any type is called every voter is sent a polling card telling them where they can vote in person and their voter number. In the UK, if you cannot vote at the polling station on election day you can apply for a postal vote, which you post in advance of the election or you appoint a proxy voter (someone else) to vote on your behalf. Voting is not compulsory in the UK.

At the polling station, usually a local school or hall, the voter is given a ballot paper. In a private booth the voter completes the ballot paper and then places it in a ballot box. After the close of the election the box is taken to a central place and opened and the votes are counted with all the other votes for all the other ballot boxes from the local area. The counting of the votes is done openly and observed by the candidates and their supporters.

> **Remember**
>
> For each of the election systems remember the term, an example of its use and its key elements.

First past the post (FPTP)

Example of its use: Electing Members of Parliament (MPs), which leads to the formation of the UK Government.

> **Remember**
>
> FPTP is currently used in UK general elections. You win by getting more votes than any other candidate.

Key elements

- MPs are currently elected using the first-past-the-post voting system.

- The country is divided into constituencies, each of which elects one MP.

- Each person over eighteen on the electoral register at the time of the election casts one vote by placing an single X on their ballot paper against the candidate of their choice.

- The candidate with the most votes is elected.

FPTP is also used to elect local government councillors in England and Wales. Sometimes more than one councillor is elected for the same area at the same time. If three are to be elected, those with the highest three voting totals are elected.

Single transferrable voting system (STV)

Example of its use: This system is used in Northern Ireland to elect Members of the European Parliament, Members of the Northern Ireland Assembly and local councillors. It has been used since 2007 in Scotland to elect local councillors.

Key elements

- The system asks voters to place candidates in rank order, i.e. 1, 2, 3, 4 and so on (1 being your first choice).

- For each electoral area, several people will be elected, so often a political party will put forward several candidates.

- A candidate is given a specific number of votes they require to be elected (quota). If they have more than the number of votes required, their extra votes are allocated to the second choices on the ballot paper.

- After all the extra votes are used up, the candidates with the smallest total of votes are eliminated and their votes redistributed.

- This type of system is called Proportional Representation. In this system the percentage of votes cast links directly to the number of candidates from a particular party being elected.

Additional member system (AMS)

Example of its use: This voting system is used to elect members of the Scottish Parliament, the Welsh Assembly and the Greater London Authority.

Key elements

- This system gives each elector two votes on the ballot paper.

- The first vote uses the FPTP system.

- The second vote is for a party list of candidates (see below).

- So each body has a certain amount of members elected by FPTP and a certain amount chosen from a list. This model of topping up members from the second vote makes the system more proportional.

Remember

STV is used in Northern Ireland for European elections. It is a proportional system, i.e. the votes for a party equate to the number of seats won. 25 per cent of the vote = 25 per cent of the seats.

Remember

AMS is used in Scottish Parliament elections.

There are two votes for two types of MP – constituency plus 'top up'.

This is a proportional system.

Example

For the first vote, the Liberal Democrats had three members elected by FPTP.

For the second vote, the total Liberal Democrat vote was 10 per cent of the total vote.

The Assembly needed a total of 60 members.

The Liberal Democrats should have six candidates in total (10 per cent) – the three members from FPTP and the top three names on the Liberal Democrats' candidate list.

Body	Members elected by FPTP	Top-up members
Scottish Parliament	73	56
Welsh Assembly	40	20
Greater London Authority	14	11

Party list system

Example of its use: This is the system used to elect Members of the European Parliament (MEPs). England, Scotland and Wales are split into regions, each of which elects several MEPs.

Key elements

- Voters cast a single vote X for a list of candidates.

- If there are seven MEPs to be elected, the Labour Party would put forward seven names for their party list.

- If the voter wanted to vote Labour, they would vote X next to the Labour list in the ballot paper.

- All the votes for each party list are counted.

- If Labour got half of the total votes cast and there were six MEPs to be elected, the top three names on the Labour list would be elected.

- The political parties decide the order of the candidates on their list. They are elected in the order decided by the political party.

Remember

Party list system is used for European elections in England, Scotland and Wales.

A single X is put on the ballot paper against a party list.

Supplementary vote (SV)

Example of its use: This system is used to elect directly elected mayors, including the Mayor of London.

Key elements

- Each voter has two votes and places a '1' against their first choice and a '2' against their second choice candidate.

- All the first choice votes are counted.

- If a candidate has a majority of the votes cast (50 per cent plus one), they are elected.

- If no candidates have a majority vote, the top two candidates remain in the race and the second choice votes of all the other candidates are redistributed.

- The winner is the candidate with the most votes after all the first and second choices are added together.

Remember

Supplementary vote is used to elect mayors – for example, in London.

Voters have two votes using a '1' and a '2'.

The top two candidates go through if no one gets 50 per cent on first count.

Second count: all other votes are redistributed.

Possible changes

In April 2011, it was proposed that FPTP be replaced with by the alternative vote (AV) system where you still elect one MP for a constituency but place your choice of candidates in rank order, i.e. 1, 2, 3, 4. If no candidate receives over 50 per cent first choice votes, the lowest placed candidates are eliminated and their second choice votes allocated. The count continues in this way until a candidates has over 50 per cent of the vote. As a result of a referendum, the proposal was **not accepted** so FPTP remained the voting system.

What is meant by the term 'fair' in regard to an election?

The specification requires you to have knowledge of the differing systems used in the UK and asks about their 'fairness and effectiveness'.

Which of the features listed below would you consider fair and which unfair in an election system? From your answers you should then be able to frame an answer to the question 'What is meant by the term 'fair' in regard to an election?'

a. Only those over 60 can vote.

b. Everybody over ten can vote.

c. Only people in work can vote.

d. Anybody from anywhere should be able to stand for election in the UK.

e. You need to pay the government £12,000 to be a candidate.

f. You can only stand for election if 1,000 people sign a petition for you to stand.

g. You can spend as much money as you like on your election campaign.

h. You are not allowed a secret vote; everybody should know how you voted.

i. You must vote or pay a fine.

j. The voting system allows candidates to sell their votes to other candidates after the votes have been counted but before a result is announced.

k. The media are not allowed to report anything about elections.

l. Once elected, you never have to be elected again and remain in office as long as you like.

Hopefully you can see that none of the examples above operates in the UK and that in regard to fairness you need to consider who can vote, who can stand for election, how the election is run, how someone is elected, the frequency of elections and the ability of the media to report on elections.

Fairness in this context is about the general nature of elections and a citizen's involvement within a democracy. There is no correct answer as the other two questions in this section indicate. You have to be able to support your point of view, but with a clear view of what is considered fair.

What is an effective voting system?

This element relates to issues such as the ability of voters to understand the voting system, the ease with which the results are decided and understood, the ability to form governments after an election, the stability of government, i.e. not needing an election every few months.

U1 Should voting be made compulsory?

Currently, voting is not compulsory in the UK. You are not required to vote in any election. In some countries, such as Australia, it is compulsory. If you don't vote in Australia you are fined.

In the UK about 60 to 70 per cent of the electorate vote in a general election and between 25 and 40 per cent vote in other elections. The profile of voters indicates that 18-to 25-year-olds are the least likely to vote and those over 65 are the most likely to vote.

Examiner tip

There is no correct answer to the question 'Should voting be made compulsory?' Citizens must arrive at their own decisions. If this question is asked, as well as taking a view, remember to support your view with some evidence.

View in favour of compulsory voting	View against compulsory voting
The crux of this issue is that if democracy and political participation are so important to our way of life, then people ought to be made to take part.	In a democracy people have the right to not participate. Democracy is about freedom of choice.

Evidence in favour of compulsory voting	Evidence against compulsory voting
<ul><li>Low turnout can lead to the election of extremists.</li><li>A citizen's duty is to take part.</li><li>Politicians can become detached from people and their needs.</li><li>Politicians only pay attention to people who vote.</li><li>Not voting could undermine democracy.</li></ul>	<ul><li>Democracy is about the freedom to choose, including the freedom to choose not to take part.</li><li>Politicians should be made to work to get people to vote for them.</li><li>There is concern about the power of the state to control its citizens.</li></ul>

U1 Should the voting age be lowered to sixteen?

In the UK you currently have to be eighteen years old to vote. This age limit was introduced in 1970, before which you had to be 21. When women were first given the vote they had to be 30 years old to vote. Different countries have different voting ages: in Brazil it is sixteen, Cuba sixteen and Sudan seventeen.

Examiner tip

There is no correct answer to the question 'Should the voting age be lowered to sixteen?' You may make valid points for or against the idea of lowering the voting age.

Evidence in favour of lowering the voting age to sixteen	Evidence against lowering the voting age to sixteen
<ul><li>Sixteen-year-olds are fully involved in society, many work and pay taxes and they have been educated to a high level.</li><li>Many decisions made by politicians impact upon young people.</li><li>Many young people are politically active through pressure groups and community activities.</li><li>People have many other legal rights at sixteen, such as the right to marry.</li></ul>	<ul><li>Sixteen-year-olds are not mature enough to vote; they are too easily persuaded and they don't understand the issues.</li><li>Many sixteen-year-olds wouldn't vote if they had the vote.</li><li>This is not something sixteen-year-olds are concerned about or campaigning for.</li></ul>

Websites

www.electoralcommission.
org.uk
www.electoral-reform.
org.uk
www.cabinetoffice.gov.
uk/resource-library/
first-past-post-and-
alternative-vote-explained

Exam practice

Unit 1, Short Course: Section B, Question 3

Read the source below and answer parts a), b) and c) which follow.

Source A

> First past the post
> Single transferrable vote
> Additional member system

a) Identify one system that uses a proportional voting system and another that is not proportional. *(2 marks)*

b) Briefly outline the advantages and disadvantages of any one of the electoral systems named in the source. *(6 marks)*

c) Make a case for compulsory voting in the UK. *(12 marks)*

Answers online   Online ☐

U3 How can citizens participate in a democracy other than by voting in elections?

Revised ☐

We have looked at voting, which is an important form of political participation, but there are other ways to participate in democracy – for example, you can get involved in campaigning for a local or national pressure group to try to bring about a change.

That involvement could be quite limited, such as making a donation, or more active, such as:

- taking part in a campaign
- raising funds
- raising awareness
- collecting names for a petition
- lobbying or writing letters
- meeting those you wish to convince
- taking part in direct action and protests
- joining a political party to bring about change
- standing for election.

Where possible, include named examples in any answers to show your understanding.

U3 | **Why should we be concerned about citizens' lack of involvement in the political process?**

Revised ☐

Many politicians are concerned about the lack of citizen involvement in the political process. Membership of political parties has been in decline, especially among young people. Young people often don't vote in elections. If the young do not become engaged in the political process, what is the future for democracy? Within any democratic society a measure of its health is the degree to which citizens are involved in society. The number of people who vote in elections has declined in the post-war period. The membership of political parties is in decline. Political parties have difficulty in raising funds to maintain their party structures. In a democracy these issues can lead to small groups or individuals having undue influence upon the political process and democracy. Some people suggest that we as taxpayers should subsidise political parties, as happens in other countries. Changing the way we elect people on our behalf has been suggested as a way forward. How are young people engaged in the political process?

- Citizenship was introduced as a curriculum subject in schools in 2003.

- Many young people are involved in political protest via a range of groups and organisations.

- A large number of young people do voluntary work and raise money for those in need.

U3 | **How are the Government and political parties attempting to deal with voter apathy and how effective have they been?**

Revised ☐

Voter apathy means that people are no longer interested in politics or voting. Several ideas have been put forward to encourage people to vote.

- It is now easier to get a postal vote. Some local elections have been 100 per cent postal vote elections.

- In other areas, voting has taken place over several days. The day could be changed from a Thursday to a Saturday when people have more time to vote.

- Others believe that by changing the voting system more people will participate. The results to date have been mixed; more people did vote in all postal elections but there has also been an increase in postal vote fraud with people voting on others' behalf or registering many names at the same address.

The issue of effectiveness means that you need to arrive at some conclusions based upon the evidence you have presented. Looking at the 2010 General Election there was a slight increase in voter turnout, but this was due to changes in the campaign like the Prime Minister/'Presidential' debates – the first time the three major party leaders debated together in front of a television audience. Local elections still have very low turnouts, as do elections to the European Parliament. There was a referendum in 2011 regarding the introduction of the AV voting system for electing MPs to Parliament, although on a low turnout the proposal was rejected. The first debate due to e-petitions has taken place on holding an EU referendum.

Remember

Do not get confused with telephone or internet voting, which are used on television programmes.

Exam practice

Unit 3, Full Course: Section B, Question 5

a) What do we mean by political participation? *(2 marks)*

Look at the image below and answer question b).

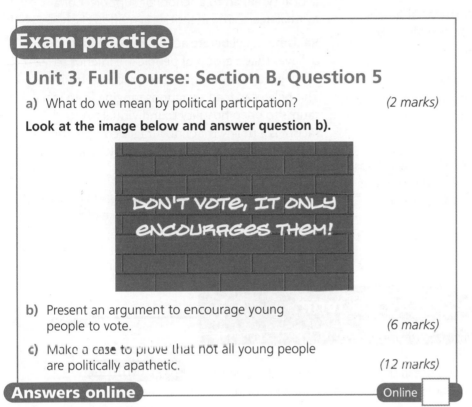

DON'T VOTe, IT ONLY eNCOURAGeS THeM!

b) Present an argument to encourage young people to vote. *(6 marks)*

c) Make a case to prove that not all young people are politically apathetic. *(12 marks)*

Answers online ——————————————— Online

2.2 How can citizens participate in democratic processes, particularly elections and voting?

2.3 The origins and implications of diversity in the United Kingdom

Key terms

Britishness – a term used to associate attributes that are linked to British 'values'.

Discrimination – unfair treatment of others based upon their race, gender, sexuality, age, disability, religion, and so on.

Identity – a sense of belonging linked to an individual through gender, sexuality, social and ethnic background, values, employment or peer group association.

Inclusion – a policy that encourages all groups within society to feel equally included and not excluded or denied access to any aspect of community life.

Multiple identities – when an individual is able to assume a range of identities, i.e. part of a family, a locality, linked to a school or supporter of a football team. The identities can often clash.

Racism – a deliberate act whereby an individual believes that a group of people are inferior to other groups based upon their race or ethnicity. This belief can lead to actions ranging from racial taunts to open hostility to individuals. Anti-racism is a policy that encourages co-operation between different racial groups i.e. Kick It Out in regard to football supporters.

Tolerance – an acceptance based upon mutual respect for others and an acceptance of things that one might disagree with.

U1 What is understood by the term 'Britishness'?

 Revised

Britishness is a belief that those who live in the UK have shared values, which should be accepted by all. This includes shared values such as fairness, justice and equality – values that are seen by many as universal but are often claimed to have their roots in British history.

The idea of discussing the nature of Britishness is a recent innovation, which has led to some debates around the following topics.

● **Integration:** the growing diversity of the population within the UK and whether individuals and groups have integrated into UK society. This debate arises from the nature of terrorism since 9/11 and the way in which UK citizens have been involved.

● **Devolution:** the growth of devolution within the UK and the concern by some politicians that the UK may break up an as entity, hence a need to stress the elements that make all of us within the UK 'British'.

Prime Minister David Cameron spoke out on the topic of integration in 2011, stressing the need for all to feel a sense of belonging to the UK and to accept British values. He criticised some past policies that did not encourage integration by immigrant groups moving into the UK in regards to issues such as the ability to speak English.

Remember

Do not confuse this debate on values with shared customs or with stereotypes such as drinking tea, standing in queues or complaining about the weather.

Examiner tip

When studying this topic it is helpful to cross-reference the UNDHR (United Nations Declaration of Human Rights), the ECHR (European Convention on Human Rights) and the HRA (Human Rights Act 1998 – UK) as well as the CRC (UN Convention on the Rights of the Child) to see how many of the claimed values associated with Britishness are universal values.

Possible changes

This concern over integration of immigrant groups and the number of immigrants arriving in the UK is a current political issue that is raised with politicians. Immigration often becomes an issue during periods of economic uncertainty. The current Government has suggested limits on the numbers of immigrants from countries outside the UK. This proposal has been criticised by some business leaders as it could affect their ability to employ skilled staff from other countries or even other parts of a multinational company.

U1 What are the constituent parts of the United Kingdom?

Revised ☐

This is a limited factual section of the specification. 'The UK' is the overarching political term to describe England, Scotland, Wales (Great Britain) and Northern Ireland.

The nature of the devolution process since 1997 has meant that each nation within the UK has differing powers and responsibilities. Note the position of Northern Ireland, which has a land border with the Irish Republic. Ireland was divided into two distinct political entities in 1921. The violence that occurred in the late 1960s led the UK Government to govern Northern Ireland by direct rule until after the Good Friday Agreement of 1998, which allowed devolved power to be granted back to the people of Northern Ireland.

Possible changes

A debate is currently taking place regarding increasing the powers devolved to the nations of the UK. This may have an impact in regard to law-making, areas of responsibility and the ability to raise money. The SNP in Scotland are pledged to hold a referendum on Scottish independence.

> **Remember**
>
> Be aware of the different terms that can be used. Often key phrases are confused such as UK, Britain, Great Britain, England, Wales, Scotland, British, Scottish, Welsh and Irish. UK will be the term mainly used in the examination. A UK passport uses the phrase United Kingdom of Great Britain and Northern Ireland.

U1 Definitions of prejudice, discrimination, stereotypes and labelling

Revised

All the terms explained below could appear on an examination paper. They have clear definitions that are applicable to citizenship. Where possible, outline a recent example to indicate that not only do you know a fact but you can understand it and explain it by the use of an example.

Prejudice – where a person has an unreasonable dislike for a person or group of people; a view not based upon experience. This term is often associated with racial views – for example, racial prejudice.

Discrimination – the act of unfairly treating others differently because of the group they belong to. This discrimination can be linked to, for example, race, sex, age and gender.

Stereotyping – a widely held generalised view about an identifiable group of people linked to a personal characteristic – for example, hair colour, where they live or a way of life.

Labelling – using a term to describe someone and therefore expecting them to behave in certain way – for example, young people are yobs and are therefore expected to exhibit a certain pattern of behaviour.

Examiner tip

Revise and rehearse the terms and ensure you use each one correctly. Remember to support your knowledge of the term with an example. This shows the examiner that you have an understanding of the term rather than just having remembered a definition.

U1 Why is tolerance important?

Revised

Tolerance is the ability to accept things you dislike or with which you disagree. In a society, this ability represents a high degree of maturity where a society or country is able to accept individuals and groups with a range of views, opinions and lifestyles and live in harmony.

Websites

http://news.bbc.co.uk/hi/english/static/in_depth/uk/2002/race
www.equalityhumanrights.com
www.telegraph.co.uk/comment/telegraph-view/3618632/Ten-core-values-of-the-British-identity.html

Test yourself

Tested

1 What do you understand by the term 'prejudice'?
2 What is the UK?
3 How does Northern Ireland differ from the rest of the UK?
4 Outline briefly one value associated with Britishness.

Quick quiz online

Exam practice

Unit 1, Short Course: Section B, Question 3

c) To what extent does discrimination still exist in the UK? *(12 marks)*

Answers online

Online

U3 What is the nature of British identity?

Revised

Social identity – the social groups to which we attach ourselves by age, gender or interest – for example, we identify with our friends at school. The nature of media in the UK means that social identity is often transmitted as a part of a national cultural identity.

Political identity – a sense of belonging to a political culture linked to the UK's shared political values – for example, a parliamentary democracy with a party system based upon universal suffrage.

Economic identity – as an individual and a family the state of our personal finances gives us both a status and identity. In terms of the UK, while there are regional differences they are not so marked that a recession or a boom will not impact upon the entire UK to some degree. The only exception to this unified economy approach is London, which appears to have a micro economy divorced from the rest of the UK, with low unemployment, high wages, high housing costs and high property costs.

Cultural identity – a sense that the media and its transmission normally cover the entire UK and are in English, which helps develop a single national identity.

> **Remember**
>
> Take care when assuming that values can be linked distinctly in the twenty-first century to specific countries. The UK fits into a larger family of countries that share certain values and characteristics, which then relate to specific values – for example, parliamentary democracy, elections, a free press, limited control of the media, free association, free movement of people, economy based upon capitalism, membership of international bodies, acceptance of the rule of law and the independence of the judiciary.

U3 Multiple identities in a diverse society

Revised

In modern society, individuals may have differing identities in different situations and with differing groups of people. For example, many people born in Cornwall relate more to a Cornish identity than a British identity. Someone from London, whose parents were born in Pakistan, watching a Test Match at Lords might have multiple identities when England are playing Pakistan.

U3 What are the opportunities and barriers to citizen participation?

Revised

This is a very broad topic so you will only need to have an outline of the nature of the issues involved. Participation in this context relates to the ability to play a full part in the life of the UK.

Barriers to citizen participation

- Language
- Access to education
- Poor housing
- Employment/unemployment
- State of health
- Disability.

Some barriers are subject to legislation in regard to anti-discrimination laws – for example, race, age, sex. There are currently three major anti-discrimination laws enforced in the UK:

● **The Sex Discrimination Act 1975 (SDA1975)** prohibits discrimination on grounds of sex and marital status.

● **The Race Relations Act 1976 (RRA 1976)** prohibits discrimination on grounds of race, colour, nationality, ethnic and national origin.

● **The Disability Discrimination Act 1995 (DDA1995)** deals with discrimination on grounds of disability.

Opportunities for citizen participation

Opportunities can be developed through the work of local authorities or the voluntary sector. The concept of the Big Society is partly concerned with encouraging citizen participation.

Exam practice

Unit 3, Full Course: Section B, Question 5

a) Give an example of two forms of discrimination.   *(2 marks)*

b) Outline ways in which the Government attempts to overcome discrimination.   *(6 marks)*

c) What changes would you propose that the Government could introduce to improve anti-discrimination policy in the UK?   *(12 marks)*

Answers online   Online

2.4 Ethnicity, identity, community life and promoting cohesion

Key terms

Community cohesion – 'Working towards a society in which there is a common vision and sense of belonging by all communities; a society in which the diversity of people's backgrounds and circumstances is appreciated and valued; a society in which similar life opportunities are available to all; and a society in which strong and positive relationships exist and continue to be developed in the workplace, in schools and the wider community.'

Guidance issued by the Government, 2007

Equal opportunities – allowing all people equality of access to opportunities throughout their lives. Often associated with government legislation to promote equality.

Ethnicity – a person's racial, religious or national grouping.

Multiculturalism – a multicultural society comprises a variety of different ethnic groups. Multiculturalism is related to a doctrine that promotes community cohesion through the celebration of different cultures and diversity within a community.

U1 How can migration shape communities?

 Revised

Make sure you know the difference between migration and immigration.

- **Migration** – the movement of people from one country to another; some moving in, others moving out.

- **Immigration** – people moving into a country.

The term **net migration** is often used in regard to the UK. It means the difference between the total number of people in and out of an area over a given period. If more people move in than leave, the figure is a plus. If more people move out, the change to the population is a minus.

Immigrants are drawn to the UK for a variety of reasons. Over the centuries the UK has seen different waves of migration, from the Romans, Saxons, Danes and Normans to more modern-day examples like Irish migration in the eighteenth and nineteenth centuries. Many have come to the UK to escape persecution or hardship in their home countries, other are termed 'economic migrants', those who come to gain employment. In the post-war period the UK Government encouraged migration to the UK from parts of the former British Empire, as there were labour and skills shortages in certain industries and services. This often led to patterns of migration where large groups of migrants from the same country moved to the same part of the UK.

An aspect of our membership of the EU is that all people living within the EU are free to move and take up work within its borders. The UK Government has limited such access for some of the newer members of the EU.

Often people migrating to the UK settle with other people from their country of origin, or they settle where specific work can be found. This has led to distinct ethnic communities developing within many urban areas. In some parts of London, new migrants to the UK settle in the areas where there are

Remember

Define the term 'migration' – the movement of population.

Examiner tip

When studying this topic, it is helpful to ensure that you have up-to-date information (see Websites on page 56). While many people have strong views regarding this topic, questions often require a balanced response. Remember that if you make a study of the changing population in your own community, this can be used in your responses to questions.

Examiner tip

In order to answer questions about this topic, study the migration patterns over the past 100 years in your own community, area and region. Migration is often linked to employment and the changing pattern of industry can also impact upon migration.

already a large number of migrants. As they become wealthier, the migrants move on to a different area and another group of migrants moves in, until they in turn prosper and move on.

Migration Watch UK, a pressure group concerned about immigration into the UK, makes the following points to support its position.

Six key facts

1. Net immigration quadrupled to 237,000 a year between 1997 and 2007. In 2009, it was 196,000. Around 3 million immigrants have arrived since 1997.

2. A migrant still arrives almost every minute.

3. We must build a new home every six minutes for new migrants.

4. England is already, with Holland, the most crowded country in Europe (except Malta).

5. Immigration will add 7 million to the population of England in the next 24 years – that is 7 times the population of Birmingham.

6. To keep the population of the UK, now 61.2 million, below 70 million, net immigration must be reduced by 50,000 a year. With balanced migration it would peak at about 65 million.

Revised September 2010

Possible changes

For up-to-date information refer to Websites. The government website gives you access to all current data regarding all aspects of life in the UK. Migration Watch is a non-political group that investigates migration issues.

> **Examiner tip**
>
> Make sure you have revised a case study relating to migration, based either upon your locality or from a national perspective. Try to make it recent, i.e. since 1945.

> **Examiner tip**
>
> Remember to research recent changes in regard to immigration and its changing patterns and current government policy.
>
> www.bbc.co.uk/news/10436228 provides background on the current government's proposals.
>
> http://news.bbc.co.uk/1/hi/uk/4218740.stm provides in map format details of recent immigration into the UK.

> **Websites**
>
> http://data.gov.uk/dataset/social_trends_41 (This site provides a complete data picture of the UK – search for the topic you wish to study) www.migrationwatchuk.org

U1 Contemporary issues relating to multiculturalism and community cohesion

 Revised

There is a range of issues that relate to living in twenty-first century Britain, and many are associated with the nature of multiculturalism and community cohesion. Some of these issues relate to everyday life: educational outcomes and access to universities; requirements changing for becoming a UK citizen; employment opportunities; the lack of cohesion in some larger urban areas where different groups often live in distinct communities.

Many politicians question the nature of integration against the celebration of multiculturalism where differing cultures are encouraged. The popular press sometimes raises broader issues such as the level of immigration and the nature of asylum.

> **Examiner tip**
>
> It is helpful if specific case studies can be mentioned in regard to these issues when answering questions. Examples can either be local or national.

> **Examiner tip**
>
> Give clear definitions in your responses and support these with examples. You do not need detailed historical knowledge of how the UK has become a multicultural society, just an overview that as a society we have always had immigration. This examination is concerned with developments since 1945.

U1 What are shared common perspectives or shared values?

Revised

What do we mean by shared perspectives and values? Are there some beliefs about what is right or wrong and what is important that are agreed upon and shared by the vast majority of society?

Some values relate to the nature of our society, others to our legal rights, and others relate to us as individuals.

Our values in society	Our values in law	Our values as individuals
• Political system • Democracy • Constitutional monarchy • Participation – citizens' involvement • A 'free' media	• What is accepted behaviour and what is unlawful • Right to justice • Legal system separate from the political system • Laws to protect citizens, e.g. discrimination, rights at work	• Right to worship freely • Rights at differing ages • Freedom of speech and association

Along with rights, remember that a citizen of a country also has responsibilities. These also must be shared by the community as a whole, such as observing the rule of law and participating within society.

The UK does not have a written constitution, unlike many other countries such as the USA, so there are a variety of sources that ensure that these shared values have validity. Many are written into law – for example, the Human Rights Act, 1988.

Examiner tip

Revise by drawing up a list with two columns: one entitled 'Rights' and the other 'Responsibilities'. Under each title, identify what you believe to be the key shared values in British society.

Remember

Usually in the UK, changes in these shared values/beliefs normally take place after a lengthy public debate where a consensus develops in favour of the change. Currently there are several ongoing debates about issues that can be called shared values – for example, the right to die, votes at sixteen, smoking bans and the legalisation of certain drugs. In 2011, the Government introduced the concept of e-petitioning whereby if 100,000 citizens sign an online petition regarding an issue it would then be discussed in Parliament.

U1 Government actions to reduce discrimination and disadvantage

Revised

Remember

The term 'government' in this context refers to the actions of the UK Central Government.

Government can take a range of actions to reduce discrimination and disadvantage. It can:

● pass legislation (laws)

● introduce regulations

● change its taxation policies

● promote issues or causes itself or provide funds to others

● work with other agencies and governments to bring about change.

At the time of a general election, political parties will often put forward ideas in their manifesto (a document containing the policies they wish to introduce) to end discrimination. Anti-discrimination policy can relate to individuals and to groups – for example, the right to a civil partnership or employment rights for older citizens.

After the Second World War, a series of welfare-related policies was introduced to help eliminate disadvantage and the range and scope of these has increased over the years. They have included a free National Health Service, a social security benefit system and free state education. In recent years, government has introduced a minimum wage for everyone and ended many age discrimination issues such as the age at which one is able to gain a pension.

In 2006, the Equality Act established a new body called the Commission for Equality and Human Rights to be the central national body to deal with discrimination issues. The list below indicates some of the legislation that has been introduced in the UK to counter discrimination:

- Disability Discrimination Acts 1995 and 2005
- Equal Pay Act 1970
- Equality Acts 2006 and 2010
- Race Relations Acts 1965, 1968, 1976 and 2000
- Representation of the People Acts 1918 and 1928
- Sex Discrimination Acts 1975 and 2002.

Test yourself
Tested

1 Identify any two pieces of anti-discrimination legislation.
2 What change took place in 2006?

Quick quiz online

Exam practice

Unit 1, Short Course: Section B, Question 3

b) Identify three ways in which communities could celebrate cultural diversity. *(6 marks)*

Answers online
Online

U3 The impact of migration
Revised

The term 'global village' is used to refer to the fact that with the ability to travel and the speed of news and 24/7 media, the world is becoming a smaller place as far as how quickly the impact of something elsewhere is felt in the UK.

The impact of immigration into the UK has had a similar effect on:

- the way we talk
- the music we like
- the latest fashions
- the food we eat.

Examiner tip
Rather than becoming an expert on all aspects of discrimination, focus your revision on one area and study our changing attitudes to discrimination, the policies and action that have been taken and whether they have been successful.

Websites
www.equalityhumanrights.com

Remember
Central Government has introduced a range of legislation since 1945 to end discrimination and disadvantage. As new forms of discrimination are recognised, new legislation has been enacted – for example, the minimum wage and equal pay.

Examiner tip
To help you revise, draw up a list of bullet points about changes in the UK that have been brought about by immigration.

We can relate all of these to different ethnic influences within the UK. It is therefore possible to consider how migration has had an effect on our cultural, social and economic life. The diversity seen at the Notting Hill Carnival each year is a testament to the cultural diversity that exists in the UK: the carnival itself is modelled upon the Rio carnival in Brazil. The growth of Reggae music and the popularity of Bollywood-style films in the UK owe much to the nature of our multi-ethnic society.

The importance of such influences is that they have crossed ethnic divides and become a part of the mainstream, and are seen as a part of the UK's identity. Think about the fast foods that we consume. How many of these have been influenced by migration into the UK?

U3 The concept of equality in a changing society

Revised

As society has evolved, our sense of the development of our rights has changed. Today, rather than legal and political rights, people are concerned about social and environmental rights. We use a much broader interpretation of the term 'equality' to cover a greater number of groups of citizens.

Some examples of groups that have campaigned in regard to equality are shown below.

Groups seeking change	Legislative changes that have taken place
Equal Rights for Women	Representation of the People Act 1928 Equal Pay Act 1970 Equality Acts 2006 and 2010 Sex Discrimination Acts 1975 and 1986 Employment Equality Regulations 2003 and 2006
Racial Equality	Race Relations Acts 1965, 1968, 1976 and 2000
Rights of the Child	The United Nations Convention on the Rights of the Child came into force on 15 January 1992. Every child in the UK is entitled to over 40 specific rights.
Sexual Rights	The Sexual Offences Act 1967 Civil Partnerships Act 2005 Sexual Offences Act 2003 The Gender Recognition Act 2004.
Disability Rights	Disability Discrimination Acts 1995 and 2005 The Special Needs and Disability Act 2001

Examiner tip

Revise at least two groups that have campaigned in regard to equality. Focus on the following aspects of the issue:

● The ways in which they believed they suffered unequal treatment

● How they campaigned for change

● The changes that have taken place.

Most importantly, include any contemporary case studies in your answer to support progress or lack of progress in regard to their equal treatment.

U3 Cohesive communities

Revised

This issue can be looked at from two different angles.

- **Looking at why some communities are cohesive**. This can be due to common shared interests, common backgrounds and a historically stable population. This style of cohesion can refer to smaller, more rural communities where little migration has taken place. The population can feel threatened when new people move into their community – for example, the issue of second homes in Wales and the South West of England.

- **Looking at where communities have successfully integrated over a period of time with a range of migrants**. These communities often celebrate the benefits that different cultures bring to a society. There are examples of good local integration. These aspects of community cohesion can be best used in the exam by the use of researched case studies of local communities.

U3 Celebrating cultural diversity

Revised

In a multicultural society, there are many examples of celebrating cultural diversity.

- Schools promote equal opportunity and diversity within their communities.

- Many local communities have formal groups established and supported by local authority funding to assist community cohesion – for example in Oldham they have established a partnership on community cohesion. The group comprises community cohesion advisors and practitioners from a range of organisations and was launched in 2006.

- Another example of a local authority sponsored event celebrating cultural diversity is the Mid Sussex Diversity Forum and Mid Sussex District Council where together they have helped to bring together local people from different cultural backgrounds for a unique event celebrating the many diverse community groups in Mid Sussex. Local community groups provided exotic food to taste, while cultural dances, songs and music were performed by residents from the Philippines, Europe, South Africa, India and Kenya. The finale was an international wedding fashion show to coincide with the Royal Wedding.

- Mid Sussex Diversity Forum has been set up as a platform to provide advice and information to support the different communities in Mid Sussex and to foster an appreciation of our rich diversity of cultures.

- The Kick It Out campaign sponsored by the Football Association is a good example of how groups have got together to end discrimination and improve community cohesion.

- The role of the media is important and television in particular is now very aware of its responsibilities in regard to labelling or stereotyping different groups.

Exam practice

Unit 3, Full Course: Section B, Question 5

a) What is meant by the term 'migration'? *(2 marks)*

b) In what ways do we in the UK benefit from being a multicultural society? *(6 marks)*

c) Devise a six-point plan to present to your local council to improve community cohesion in your local area. *(12 marks)*

Answers online ─────────────── Online ☐

The topic to be pre-released could state:

Theme 2 – Being a citizen in the UK: Democracy and identity
Topic – Migration, multiculturalism and community cohesion.

If there are three topics given, it is reasonable to think that as there are three questions, there will be a question on each topic. Practise preparing for a part c) extended writing response worth 12 marks, using the topic given above – Migration, multiculturalism and community cohesion. The question will be similar to this one, but insert the correct word from the pre-released topic:

Present a case to outline the benefits of _____ to the UK *(12 marks)*.
Complete an outline plan for your response in the form of a spider chart.
Make sure you do this for your pre-released topic before your exam.

Examiner tip

Pre-released topic.

While the actual questions are not known until you enter the examination room, the Awarding Body makes available the title of the topic to be answered.

3.1 What are my rights and responsibilities as a British citizen within a broader framework of human rights?

Key terms

Citizenship – where an individual is fully recognized by a state as being a member of that state. It is a legal concept that gives a legal status to the citizen, granting certain rights but also certain responsibilities.

Civil liberties – rights and freedoms that protect an individual citizen from the state. Civil liberties set limits on what a government can do so that it cannot abuse its power or interfere unduly with the lives of private citizens.

Duties (responsibilities) – as well as gaining rights as a citizen, states also expect citizens to perform certain duties – for example, in time of war a nation may conscript citizens into the armed forces.

ECHR – the European Convention on Human Rights is an international treaty to protect human rights and freedom in Europe. The Convention was drafted in 1950 by the Council of Europe and came into force in September 1953. All Council of Europe member states are bound to the Convention. The UK Government was a founder signatory to the Convention. UK citizens can take cases to the European Court of Human Rights.

Human rights – these are basic rights and freedoms to which all people are entitled. Since the end of the Second World War, these rights have been written into a large number of international charters (see page 63).

Human Rights Act (HRA) 1998 – this incorporated the European Convention on Human Rights fully into UK law. It allowed UK courts to decide upon many issues regarding the Convention without having to refer cases to the European Court of Human Rights.

UNDHR – the UN General Assembly adopted the United Nations Declaration of Human Rights (UNDHR) in December 1948 and for the first time there was an agreed statement of the rights to which all human beings were entitled.

UN Convention on the Rights of the Child – in 1989, governments worldwide agreed to adopt the UN Convention on the Rights of the Child (CRC). The Convention stated the basic rights in regard to children; what a child needs to survive, grow, participate and reach their potential. The Convention applies equally to every child, regardless of who they are, or where they are from.

U1 Citizens' rights and responsibilities in the UK

Revised

The Magna Carta was signed in 1215, and from this came the idea of basic legal rights. Since then, there has been a series of developments to increase the rights of citizens and to lay down civic responsibilities.

At different periods in our history, different types of rights have emerged to take prominence in public debate.

From Magna Carta, 1215 there began the development of basic **legal rights**:

- the right to a free trial
- the use of juries
- not being arrested without reason.

Campaigns regarding **religious rights** continued into the nineteenth century. Male Roman Catholics were only given the vote in 1829, and in 1832 the first major reform of who could vote and the size and distribution of parliamentary seats took place.

As the UK became an industrial society in the nineteenth century, campaigns took place to develop **economic rights** – for example, the right to form and join a trade union. In 1834, some farm labourers from Dorset, known as the Tolpuddle Martyrs, were sent as convict prisoners to Australia because they swore an illegal oath on joining an agricultural workers' trade union.

In recent years, **rights** relating to a citizen's **personal life** have become the basis for changes in law – for example, equal opportunities legislation, equal pay and issues relating to sexuality such as homosexual law reform and the concept of civil partnership.

From this grew a call for **political rights** with major changes taking place in the nineteenth and twentieth centuries with the right to vote. Women did not get the right to vote until 1918, when they could vote at the age of 28, and they only got the vote at 21 in 1928. The voting age was lowered from 21 to 18 in 1971.

In the twentieth century, the idea of **welfare rights** developed in the UK. Citizens now have an expectation that certain services and benefits are provided for everyone – for example, education, health care, pensions and unemployment benefit.

There are currently growing calls in regard to rights concerning **global issues** and **environmental issues**.

The rights of a UK citizen

- The right to life.
- Freedom from torture and degrading treatment.
- Freedom from slavery and forced labour.
- The right to liberty.
- The right to a fair trial.
- The right not to be punished for something that was not a crime when you did it.
- The right to respect for privacy and family life.
- Freedom of thought, conscience and religion, and freedom to express your beliefs.

- Freedom of expression.
- Freedom of assembly and association.
- The right to marry and start a family.
- The right not to be discriminated against in respect of these rights and freedoms.
- The right to peaceful enjoyment of your property.
- The right to an education.
- The right to participate in free elections.
- The right not to be subjected to the death penalty.

If your rights are threatened, you are able to seek a solution through the courts. Most rights have limits to ensure that they do not unfairly damage other people's rights.

If you are a citizen of a country, you also have responsibilities as well as rights; they include the responsibility to obey the law, pay your taxes, respect the rights of others. You have individual responsibility for your own care and that of your family. You accept that the state can control your freedoms in some circumstances, i.e. conscription in the case of a war.

Possible changes

Many people in society think that some people are more concerned about their rights than their responsibilities. Others feel that the Human Rights Act, 1988, needs reform and should be replaced with a UK Bill of Rights.

The United Nations Convention on the Rights of the Child

This was agreed in September 1990 and as of November 2009, 194 countries had agreed to abide by the Convention. The Convention places a duty on governments in regard to the following areas in relation to children:

● The right to life.

● The right to his or her own name and identity.

● The right to be protected from abuse or exploitation.

● The right to an education.

● The right to having their privacy protected.

● The right to be raised by, or have a relationship with, their parents.

● The right to express their opinions and have these listened to and, where appropriate, acted upon.

● The right to play and enjoy culture and art in safety.

Remember

- Human rights are based on key documents such as the UNDHR.
- In the UK, the HRA (1998) is the key document, outlining a citizen's basic human rights.
- UK citizens have the right to appeal their case to the European Court of Human Rights.
- Rights have developed over time, and at different periods in our history different types of rights have emerged to take prominence in public debate.

Websites

www.udhr.org/history/
www.echr.coe.int/echr/homepage_EN
www.justice.gov.uk/guidance/docs/act-studyguide.pdf

Revised

The United Nations Declaration of Human Rights, 1948 is the key legislation in regard to the recent development of human rights. It is made up of 30 elements.

1. We are all born free and equal.
2. Don't discriminate.
3. The right to life.
4. No slavery.
5. No torture.
6. You have rights no matter where you go.
7. We are all equal before the law.
8. Your human rights are protected by law.
9. No unfair detention.
10. The right to trial.
11. We are always innocent till proven guilty.
12. The right to privacy.
13. Freedom of movement.
14. The right to seek a safe place to live.
15. The right to a nationality.
16. Marriage and family.
17. The right to your own things.
18. Freedom of thought.
19. Freedom of expression.
20. The right to public assembly.
21. The right to democracy.
22. The right to housing, education and child care and help if you are old or ill.
23. Rights to a job, a fair wage and membership of a trade union.
24. The right to rest from work and to relax.
25. Food and shelter for all.
26. The right to education.
27. Copyright protection of your ideas and inventions.
28. A fair and free world.
29. Responsibility: we have a duty to other people, and we should protect their rights and freedoms.
30. No one can take away your human rights.

The European Convention on Human Rights (ECHR), 1953 – the Convention for the Protection of Human Rights and Fundamental Freedoms, known as the European Convention on Human Rights, came into force in September 1953.

The Convention ensured the rights stated in the United Nations Declaration of Human Rights came into effect in European countries, and established an international court with powers to find fault against states that do not fulfil their undertakings. The court sits in Strasbourg, France, and is made up of judges from each of the member countries. The UK was one of the first countries to agree to the ECHR. The Convention has been updated several times since 1953.

The Human Rights Act, 1998 – this act ensured that the European Convention on Human Rights was embedded in UK law. This meant that UK citizens could bring cases before UK courts and have them resolved without having to go to the court in Strasbourg. It also meant that UK courts had to abide by and take account of decisions of the Court in Strasbourg when arriving at their own decisions. It also stated that UK public bodies had to abide by the Convention.

Remember

Do not confuse the European Court of Human Rights with the European Court, which is the court of the EU (European Union), or state that the Court is linked to the EU. It is an entirely separate body.

3.1 What are my rights and responsibilities as a British citizen within a broader framework of human rights?

AQA GCSE Citizenship Studies 65

U1 Case studies: human rights abuse

Revised

With the United Nations, the international community has established means whereby individuals responsible for human rights abuse can be held to account.

Case studies

- At the end of the Second World War, the Allies set up the Nuremberg and Tokyo trials where individuals and organisations were charged with war crimes, crimes against peace and crimes against humanity.

- In the 1990s, International Criminal Tribunals for the former Yugoslavia and for Rwanda were set up by international agreement.

- In 1998, 120 countries signed the Rome Statute, which established a permanent **International Criminal Court (ICC)**. The court sits at The Hague in Holland.

- To date, the ICC has opened investigations into six cases regarding alleged abuses in the Democratic Republic of the Congo, the Central African Republic, Uganda, Sudan, Kenya and Libya.

Concerned citizens

Bodies such as Amnesty International campaign to stop human rights abuse by highlighting what is happening in the world and asking ordinary citizens to support their campaigns. Some of Amnesty's current campaigns are women's rights (they champion the rights of women and girls and are holding governments accountable for ending discrimination and inequality), campaigning against the death penalty, and supporting change in North Africa and the Middle East.

Liberty is a UK-based pressure group which campaigns about civil rights in the UK. It is currently campaigning about control orders, extradition and torture.

Possible changes

Ensure that the examples you use when discussing human rights campaigns are contemporary and still matters of concern.

Test yourself

Tested

1 What type of case would be heard by the International Criminal Court?
2 Why is the UNDHR important?
3 Identify two rights of UK citizens.

Quick quiz online

Exam practice

Unit 1, Short Course: Section B, Question 4

b) Outline the benefits of two human rights enjoyed
by UK citizens.

(6 marks)

Answers online — Online

U3 Getting the balance right on human rights — Revised

There has to be a balance struck between the power of the state and the
rights and duties of its citizens. At times, this balance is brought into question.

● In the UK the police have powers of 'stop and search', but many ethnic
minority community members complain that they are subject to the use
of these powers more than other groups.

● After the 9/11 terrorist attacks in New York, new security measures were
introduced at airports. This was done with public approval.

● In Northern Ireland in the 1970s, judges decided the outcome of cases as
it was not possible to hold jury trials.

With every right there is a corresponding duty. For example, your freedom
of expression could be hurtful to others. Your freedom to hold a march may
need police permission.

U3 The balance between rights and responsibilities — Revised

A debate is currently taking place in the UK regarding the balance between
a citizen's rights and responsibilities. Some believe that citizens are more
concerned about their rights than responsibilities to society.

This is an area where you have to use your own judgement. Below are
examples of the types of questions that are asked as a part of the rights versus
responsibilities debate.

● Not everybody bothers to vote so should it be made compulsory or
should you have the freedom not to take part? What would happen if
only a very small number took part?

● Should those who receive welfare benefits have to work or carry out
community tasks in exchange? To what extent can you be a citizen of a
society but opt out of the duties of being a citizen?

Exam practice

Unit 1, Full Course: Section B

a) What is the difference between a right and a
responsibility?

(2 marks)

Answers online — Online

3.2 How are citizens' lives affected by the law?

Key terms

Civil law – law that deals with disputes between individuals or groups. There are distinct civil courts, which award damages (a money payment) or can make orders stating that certain actions should take place – for example, adoption and divorce.

Civil liberties – rights and freedoms that protect an individual citizen from the state. Civil liberties set limits on what a government can do so that it cannot abuse its power or interfere unduly with the lives of private citizens.

Criminal law – law that deals with individuals who break the law, as determined by the state. The police gather evidence and make arrests. The state prosecutes in a criminal court where juries decide whether the individual is innocent or guilty and judges determine the sentence to be given to the individual.

Crown – the monarchy, but its powers have been transfered to the state or government.

Crown Prosecution Service (CPS) – a government body that checks the evidence presented by the police and decides whether a case can be brought to court. The CPS then represents the state in court and prosecutes the accused.

Equality – treating every person equally.

Fairness – treating people fairly.

Freedom – the power or right to act, speak or think as one wants.

Judges – these are appointed by the Crown. Vacancies are advertised and are open to both solicitors and barristers. Judges either sit alone or with others in a court to hear a case. They then sum up the evidence for a jury. If the individual is convicted, they pass the sentence.

Juries – these are composed of twelve local citizens whose names are chosen at random from the list of electors. They mainly sit in criminal cases. In recent years it has become more difficult to avoid jury service, which is unpaid. The jury in a case listens to the evidence and decides whether the individual is innocent or guilty.

U1 The differences between civil and criminal law

Revised

Criminal law	Civil law
The CPS, on behalf of the state, initially decides whether a case takes place.	Individuals bring cases or disputes against other individuals.
The case is initially heard in a Magistrates' Court.	The case is heard in a County Court.
If the offence is serious, it is referred to a Crown Court.	The case can be later dealt with in the High Court.
Punishments can involve a custodial sentence (imprisonment) or non-custodial sentence such as a fine.	Damages are awarded in the form of a money award, or an order is passed stating that certain actions should take place.

County courts can deal with a wide range of civil cases, but the most common ones are:

● landlord and tenant disputes – for example, possession (eviction), rent arrears, repairs

● consumer disputes – for example, faulty goods or services

- personal injury claims (injuries caused by negligence) – for example, traffic accidents, falling into holes in the pavement, accidents at work

- undefended divorce cases and proceedings to end a registered civil partnership

- race, sex and disability discrimination cases

- discrimination cases

- debt problems – for example, a creditor seeking payment

- employment problems – for example, wages or salary owing or pay in lieu of notice.

Criminal offences are those that break the law of the land, such as murder, robbery, drunk driving or theft. See Websites for a site giving a full list of UK criminal offences.

Possible changes

It has been proposed that in some complex cases, such as company fraud, it is better for the judge to decide the verdict rather than a jury.

Remember

- Criminal law is an offence against the laws of the state.
- Civil law is concerned with disputes between individuals.
- The cases are heard in different courts.
- Most serious criminal cases are decided by juries.
- Most civil cases are decided by a judge.
- The punishments vary.

Websites

List of criminal offences in the UK:
www.legalservices.gov.uk/docs/cds_main/List_of_criminal_offences.pdf

Examiner tip

When revising, try to remember the difference between the two types of law by having some case studies to which you can refer. A celebrity's divorce is a civil case; a robbery is a criminal case.

Use the specific terms: a solicitor instructs the barrister, who is the specialist representing a person in court. Do not use generic terms, such as lawyer.

U1 Legal rights in society

Revised

A person's rights in society cover every aspect of living in contemporary Britain.

- You have a right to education from age four to sixteen.

- You have the right of access to free medical treatment.

- You have a wide range of legal rights if you are suspected of committing a crime.

- You have the right to marry at eighteen (at sixteen with your parents' consent).

- You have the right to a range of forms of protection when working, from a minimum wage to health and safety protection.

- You have the right to a range of state-provided services and benefits.

Possible changes

There is a current political debate as to whether the Human Rights Act, 1998, should be replaced with a UK Bill of Rights.

Examiner tip

When revising, remember a few clear examples of specific rights rather than having a general view. Try to relate the idea of rights to issues that impact on your daily life. This enables you to relate to them more easily.

Examiner tip

To revise this section, create a case study of an individual travelling through life, and what they can legally do at each stage.

Websites

Rights of the Child (UK):
www.direct.gov.uk/en/Parents/ParentsRights/DG_4003313

U1 How the civil law can have an impact on young people

The following table shows a range of rights of young people at different ages. These legal rights have developed over time.

Age	Legal rights You can ...
13	Work subject to certain restrictions.
14	Go into a pub, but you cannot drink or buy alcohol.
16	Leave school (it is planned to raise the school-leaving age to 18). Work full time, up to 40 hours a week. Hold a licence to drive a moped. Drink wine or beer with a meal in a restaurant. Get married with your parents' consent. Become sexually active. Buy a pet (but you must have an adult with you). Purchase a lottery ticket. Choose your own doctor. Apply for certain state benefits.
17	Hold a licence to drive any vehicle except HGVs. Purchase an air rifle.
18	Drink and purchase alcohol. Purchase tobacco. Get married (no consent required). Get a credit card. Appear in an adult court. Vote in elections. Change your name. Apply for a passport. Own land. Sit on a jury. Stand for election. Gamble. Enter into a contract (for example, for a mobile phone). Donate blood.

Civil law cases involving divorce affect a number of young people because of the issues that arise about where the young person will live. Increasingly, the wishes of the young people are taken into account when such decisions are made. Civil laws also relate to young people when they are purchasing goods as they are protected as consumers.

In recent years, some young people have been subject to Anti-Social Behaviour Orders (ASBOs). These have now been replaced by Criminal Behaviour Orders, which can be given after criminal conviction. Community Protection Orders can be brought by local authorities to stop anti-social behaviour.

Test yourself

Tested

1 Identify two ways a civil case differs from a criminal case.
2 Identify a right given to a sixteen-year-old.
3 Which age-related right would you change? Give reasons for your answer.
4 The idea of giving sixteen-year-olds the vote was in some political party manifestoes at the last general election. Can you make a case for or against this idea?

Quick quiz online

Exam practice

Unit 1, Short Course: Section B, Question 4

a) Identify two ways in which criminal law differs
from civil law.   *(2 marks)*

Answers online ——————————————————— Online

Examiner tip

The exam practice question asks for two differences so it is important to highlight the differences.

U3 Effectiveness of equal opportunities legislation

Revised

In recent years, the Government has passed a wide range of legislation to encourage equal opportunities in society.

● The Equal Pay Act 1970 amended 1983

● The Sex Discrimination Act 1975 amended 1986

● Disability Discrimination Act 1995

● The Disability Discrimination Act 2005

● The Special Educational Needs and Disability Act 2001

● Race Relations Act 1976 amended 2000

● Employment Equality Regulations 2003, 2006

● Human Rights Act 1998

In 2007, the Government merged a wide range of government bodies dealing with equal opportunities into a new body called the Equality and Human Rights Commission. It has a legal duty to promote and monitor human rights, and to protect, enforce and promote equality in regard to age, disability, gender, race, religion and belief, pregnancy and maternity, marriage and civil partnership, sexual orientation and gender reassignment.

Websites

Visit the Equality and Human Rights Commission website when revising to look for current case studies: www.equalityhumanrights.com

U3 Case studies: equal opportunities legislation

Revised

The Equality and Human Rights Commission is currently investigating the position of Gypsies and Travellers in the UK. The following facts relate to Gypsies and Travellers.

● Life expectancy for Gypsy and Traveller men and women is ten years lower than the national average.

● Gypsy and Traveller mothers are twenty times more likely than the rest of the population to have experienced the death of a child.

● In 2003, fewer than 25 per cent of Gypsy and Traveller children obtained five GCSEs and A*–C grades, compared to a national average of over 50 percent.

The Equality and Human Rights Commission is also undertaking an inquiry into disability-related harassment and how well public authorities are currently dealing with this.

Websites

When revising, look for more examples of the work of the Equality and Human Rights Commission on their website (**www.equalityhumanrights.com**). It is also helpful to look at pressure group websites that are concerned with equality issues to gain a different viewpoint, for example Disability Action: **www.disabilityaction.org**.

Exam practice

Unit 3, Full Course: Section B Question 4

b) Outline a case for equality legislation. *(6 marks)*

Answers online _____ Online [ ]

3.3 How effective is the criminal justice system?

Key terms

Custodial sentence – a sentence passed by a court that involves the accused having their freedom taken away by being placed in a prison.

Justice – the administration of the law, which is considered, fair and morally right.

Law – a system of rules recognised by a country or society as the way in which people should behave and the sanctions that can be used.

Non-custodial sentence – a sentence passed by a court that does not involve a prison sentence – for example, probation. The convicted person is still free to live in the community.

Police – an official state organisation responsible for preventing and solving crimes and maintaining public order. The police force in the UK is organised on a regional basis.

Restorative justice – brings those affected by a crime together with those responsible for the crime. Those who committed the crime are also expected, where possible, to repair any damage or make amends to the person who suffered.

Rule of law – this means that the law applies to everyone, even politicians, judges, the police and the very wealthy.

Sentencing – the process of giving a punishment to a person found guilty in a court case.

Verdict – the decision made by magistrates or a jury regarding the guilt or innocence of the accused.

> **Examiner tip**
>
> When answering a question, always add a clear example that indicates to the examiner that you understand the term. Where possible, the example should be recent and UK-based. Do not confuse the UK justice system with that of the USA.

U1 The purposes of criminal law and its role in society and the community

Revised

'The purpose of the criminal justice system is to deliver justice for all, by convicting and punishing the guilty and helping them to stop offending, while protecting the innocent. It is responsible for detecting crime and bringing it to justice; and carrying out the orders of court, such as collecting fines, and supervising community and custodial punishment.'

(An extract of a presentation by Jon Collins, Campaign Director of the Criminal Justice Alliance, to the Centre for Parliamentary Studies on 18 May 2010.)

The criminal law system has a range of components.

- The **legislature** (Parliament) decides on the law and determines Acts of Parliament (Acts to create new laws or make changes to existing laws).

- The **police force** upholds the law. It arrests suspects and gathers evidence.

> **Examiner tip**
>
> Revise this area by thinking about an imaginary island and establishing laws for the first time.
>
> - Why do you need laws?
> - What bodies do you need to uphold and enforce the law?
> - How do you deal with those who break the law?
> - What role should the ordinary citizen play in the various processes?

- The **Crown Prosecution Service** (CPS) decides whether a prosecution should go ahead and prosecutes the case on our behalf.

- **Court hearings** involve citizens sitting on a jury who then decide the guilt or innocence of the accused, and judges who decide the sentence.

- The **prison service** and **probation service** are responsible for those found guilty of an offence.

All the elements are important in the judicial process. Imagine if any one of these elements were not present. What would the consequence be for society (laws but no police force, or courts but no forms of punishment)?

Possible changes

While many people dispute the effectiveness of elements of the processes involved in criminal law, the key building blocks are not disputed.

Remember

The role that the citizen plays within the criminal justice system: concerned citizen, neighbourhood watch member, special constable, jury member and magistrate.

The key building blocks of the criminal justice system: making the law, enforcing the law, the justice system holding people to account for their actions, sanctions and sentencing enforcement.

Websites

www.restorativejustice.org.uk
www.nacro.org.uk/
www.prisonreformtrust.org.uk/
www.justice.gov.uk/guidance/prison-probation-and-rehabilitation/index.htm
www.judiciary.gov.uk/about-the-judiciary

Examiner tip

Where possible, use a case study from a recent event to demonstrate your understanding of the criminal justice system when answering questions on this topic.

U1 The law and young offenders

Revised

Those who are seventeen or under are classified as 'young offenders' and are dealt with by the youth justice system. Imprisonment for these offenders is seen as a last resort.

- Children below the age of ten are not considered to be criminally responsible for their actions and cannot be charged.

- Children aged ten to fourteen can be convicted of a criminal offence if it can be proved that they were aware that what they were doing was seriously wrong.

- After the age of fourteen, young people are considered to be fully responsible for their own actions.

When young people first commit minor offences, such as forms of anti-social behaviour, they are dealt with outside the court system. For second minor offences, they are likely to receive police final warnings or reprimands.

Youth Courts

- Youth Courts are located inside Magistrates' Courts.

- They are less formal in layout and proceedings than adult courts.

- They deal with almost all cases involving people under eighteen.

- The magistrates and district judges in these courts are able to give detention and training orders for up to 24 months as well as a range of community sentences.

- Members of the public are not able to attend Youth Courts.

- In very serious cases, a young person will appear in a Crown Court. This can occur when the offence can only be dealt with by a Crown Court – for murder, rape and robbery. The Youth Court could also decide that the punishments it has are insufficient and refer the case to the Crown Court for sentencing.

Case study: the case of James Bulger

The case of the killers of James Bulger highlights a number of points regarding dealing with young offenders.

February 1993: James Bulger, aged two, was abducted from a shopping centre in Bootle. James' battered body was later discovered by a local railway line. Jon Venables and Robert Thompson were arrested by the police for the murder of James. They were both aged ten.

November 1999: Venables and Thompson were convicted and sentenced to at least eight years of secure Youth Accommodation.

December 1999: The ECHR decided that the two did not receive a fair trial because the case was heard in an adult court and because of the way in which they had been questioned by the prosecution.

October 2000: The Lord Chief Justice ruled that Thompson and Venables could apply for parole.

June 2001: Thompson and Venables were freed on Life Licences. This means whilst they are free to lead a normal life, if they break the conditions of their licence they can be recalled to prison to complete the rest of their original sentence.

March 2010: The Ministry of Justice announced that Jon Venables had been returned to prison for an unspecified violation of the terms of his licence of release.

Possible changes

In light of the UK riots during the summer of 2011, which involved looting and arson in inner cities, the Government focused on why these incidents occurred and what were the lessons to be learned. A great deal of media coverage focused upon the number of very young people involved. Carry out some internet research on news websites to look for any comments on the UK riots, and whether there were any changes in government policy or initiatives.

Test yourself

Tested

1. At what age are you legally held to be criminally responsible?
2. Identify one aim of sentencing.
3. What is 'restorative justice'?

Quick quiz online

Exam practice

Unit 1, Short Course: Section B, Question 4

c) Present a case to the Government for lowering the age of criminal responsibility.

(12 marks)

Answers online

Online

Examiner tip

Use case studies from either national or local sources to support any points you make when answering questions on this topic.

Websites

www.prisons.org.uk

Remember

- Remember the key ages of ten, fourteen and seventeen when considering offences committed by young people.
- Youth Courts are different to adult Magistrates' Courts.
- Young people are sentenced differently to adults.

Examiner tip

This exam practice answer requires a short essay response, which it is helpful to plan by making notes before you start writing. Don't put a line through your notes – the examiner can look at them if they are not crossed through and if you run out of time can take account of them when awarding marks.

Key people and structures in the legal system

- **Solicitors** are legally qualified people who advise clients on a wide range of issues, such as divorce, buying a house, making a will, civil disputes and criminal matters. They represent clients in the lower courts, and prepare cases for barristers to try in higher courts. The function of a solicitor is parallel in medical terms to that of a family doctor/GP.

- **Barristers** are specialist legal counsels who are employed through solicitors to offer specialist legal advice or represent clients in the higher courts. The medical parallel is when your GP refers you to a specialist for your specific disorder.

- **Magistrates** are ordinary citizens who volunteer to become magistrates. Following an interview they receive training. In court they sit with other magistrates and decide the outcome of cases in Magistrates' Courts. Magistrates also sit alongside district judges in certain cases.

- **Juries** are groups of twelve citizens, randomly selected from the electoral register. They have been shortlisted to hear a case in a court located in their own area. They jointly determine the verdict of the case, making a decision based on the facts and evidence, in consultation with the judge regarding the rules of law. Juries are normally expected to reach a unanimous verdict, but judges can allow them to reach a majority verdict with one or two jurors disagreeing with the majority.

- **Judges**, collectively known as the judiciary, are qualified barristers, or in some cases solicitors who apply and after interview become either part-time recorders or full-time judges. A recorder is a part-time judge. They are normally barristers who continue in practice, for example Cherie Booth QC, wife of the former Prime Minister Tony Blair, is a recorder. Different types of courts require different categories of judge from district judges to Supreme Court judges. They are responsible for the conduct of a case and give a summary of the evidence to the jury before it retires to decide the verdict. The judge decides upon the sentence if the accused is found guilty.

- **Youth Offending Teams** develop a range of services targeted at young people who have committed offences, or who may be at risk of doing so. Youth Offending Teams make young offenders face up to the consequences of their behaviour. The service seeks to turn young offenders away from crime towards more constructive activities. They tackle issues such as poor parental supervision, truancy, school exclusion and substance misuse, which can place young people at risk of becoming involved in crime. The team is made up of professionals from a variety of agencies, including the probation service and social services.

- **The probation service** is locally based and works with offenders aged eighteen and over who have been sentenced by the courts to a Community Order or a Suspended Sentence Order, or released on licence from prison to serve the rest of their sentence in the community. Probation officers prepare pre-sentence reports for judges and magistrates in the courts, which help them to choose the most appropriate sentence. Probation officers also liaise with the victims of crime if the offender has been given a prison sentence of twelve months or longer. They work with offenders in the community to help them to stop committing further crimes. They manage approved premises (hostels) for offenders with a residence requirement (where you have to live at a certain address) on their sentences or licences. They also work in prisons, assessing offenders to prepare them for release.

- Her Majesty's **prison service** serves the public by keeping in custody those committed by the courts.

Prisons are divided into different categories according to the type of prisoners they hold.

Category A prisoners are those whose escape would be highly dangerous to the public or national security.

Category B prisoners are those who do not require maximum security, but for whom escape needs to be made very difficult.

Category C prisoners are those who cannot be trusted in open conditions but who are unlikely to try to escape.

Category D prisoners are those who can be reasonably trusted not to try to escape. This type of prison is called an open prison while the others are called closed prisons.

Young offenders and juveniles

When offenders under the age of 21 are sentenced to a custodial term, they may be sent to one of four types of establishment.

Secure Training Centres (STCs)	Privately run, education-focused centres for offenders up to the age of seventeen.
Local authority secure children's homes	Run by social services departments.
Juvenile prisons	Run by the prison service, these prisons accommodate fifteen- to eighteen-year-olds.
Young Offender Institutions (YOIs)	Run by the prison service, and accommodate eighteen- to twenty-one-year-olds.

Examiner tip

It is important to know about each of the key people and structures. You could pair them together to make comparisons and to remember the differences – for example, solicitor/barrister; magistrate/judge.

Remember

You need to know how citizens are involved in the criminal justice system, and why. Think about juries and magistrates.

U3 The purposes and practice of sentencing

Revised

According to the Criminal Justice Act, 2003, the purpose of sentencing people convicted of a crime has five elements.

1. The **punishment** of the offender.

2. Seeking to reduce crime – **deterrence**.

3. The **reform** and **rehabilitation** of the offender.

4. **Protection** for the community.

5. **Reparation** by the offender to people affected by their offences.

All sentences given by a court reflect a combination of these elements. In recent years, the fifth element has become more important and is called 'restorative justice'. Restorative justice requires offenders to meet the victims of their crime, and allows statements by victims to be taken into account by judges before passing sentence.

Remember

Learn the roles of the following: Youth Offending Team, probation service, prison service. Role means 'what they do'.

U3 The effectiveness of the criminal justice system

Revised

In relation to the effectiveness of the system you need to consider the nature of policing: sentencing and prisons.

Police – How effective are the police? How do you measure crime? Official statistics released by the police indicate that major crimes have a high clear-up rate, while many minor crimes have low conviction rates. Does the way a police force polices their local area impact on their effectiveness? How do the police relate to their local communities?

Sentencing – whilst guidance is issued to judges and magistrates they still have a degree of discretion but the government can ask for sentences to be reviewed, as can those convicted. Many are concerned at the length of time court cases can take and the costs involved; equally in regard to the summer 2011 riots some have criticised the speed at which the courts dealt with those accused.

Does prison work?

- Prisoners serving less than a year have the highest re-offending rate.

- Nearly half of prisoners released from prison go on to commit further offences.

- The National Audit Office has estimated that re-offending in England and Wales costs the taxpayer up to £10 billion a year.

All these points need to be considered when you weigh up the effectiveness of the system.

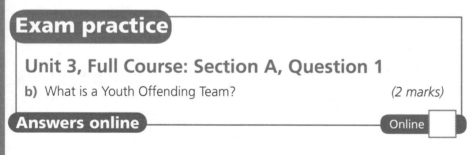

Exam practice

Unit 3, Full Course: Section A, Question 1

b) What is a Youth Offending Team? *(2 marks)*

Answers online — Online

Examiner tip

Remember when answering a question that effectiveness in regards to sentencing and prison is normally measured by the lack of re-offending – an offender not caught committing another offence within a fixed time after release.

The latest figures for re-offending are available from **www.statistics.gov. uk/hub/crime-justice/ offenders/re-offending- and-criminal-careers.**

3.4 Why does the media matter and how influential is it?

Key terms

Censorship – suppression of materials, publications and thoughts.

Freedom of the press – a concept that states that for a free, open and democratic society to exist the press should be free from political and judicial interference and be able to print the stories they wish.

Mass media – communicating to a large audience at the same point in time. Media consists of several different types of communications: television, radio, newspapers, magazines and websites.

New media – a broad term that emerged in the later part of the twentieth century that relates to the development of internet-related means of communication. New media holds out a possibility of on-demand access to content any time, anywhere, on any digital device, as well as interactive user feedback, citizen participation and community formation around the media content.

Ofcom – Office of the Regulator for Communications. This is a government-established independent regulator and competition authority for the UK communications industries.

Press Complaints Commission (PCC) – an independent self-regulatory body, which deals with complaints about the editorial content of newspapers and magazines and their websites.

Social media – this can take many different forms, including internet forums, weblogs, social blogs, microblogging, wikis, podcasts, photographs or pictures, video, rating sites and social bookmarking. These all enable citizens to control their own news agenda without referring to the traditional media.

U1 What is a 'free press' and why is it important?

Revised ☐

Do not confuse a 'free press' with free newspapers. Free newspapers are newspapers that are given away free of charge. A free press, or freedom of the press, is a concept that states that for a free, open and democratic society to exist the press should be free from political and judicial interference and be able to print the stories they wish. Clearly within any society there need to be laws to protect individuals from newspapers printing false stories, but restrictions upon the press should be limited. The term 'free press' is now more widely interpreted to mean freedom of any form of mass media.

Television in the UK is governed by legislation and has to be politically impartial; a formal charter governs the BBC. There is no requirement upon newspapers to be politically impartial. In fact, during elections political parties look to newspapers to support their cause (see page 82).

Possible changes

A government inquiry under Lord Justice Leveson was set up in July 2011 to investigate phone hacking accusations against the press. It aimed to look into the role and responsibility of the media. Carry out some internet research to find out what evidence was given to the inquiry.

> **Examiner tip**
>
> When answering questions on this topic it is helpful to have a few case studies about the freedom of the press to use as examples. The example of the *Daily Telegraph* and its disclosures regarding the claims of UK MPs indicate how much we as citizens gain by having a free press.

> **Websites**
>
> www.barb.co.uk
> www.pcc.org.uk/index.html

U1 What are the responsibilities of the media?

Revised

Newspapers and magazines operate within the Code of Practice issued by the Press Complaints Commission (PCC).

The main headings of the code relate to:

- accuracy
- opportunity to reply
- privacy
- harassment
- intrusion into grief or shock
- children
- children in sex cases
- hospitals
- reporting of crime
- using clandestine devices and subterfuge
- victims of sexual assault
- discrimination
- financial interests
- confidential sources
- witness payments in criminal trials
- payments to criminals.

There can be some exceptions to the guidance where an article is believed to be in the public interest.

There needs to be a balance between a free press and a responsible press. Do more legal controls restrict a free press? Or does a free press lead to issues such as phone hacking, which have arisen in recent years during which we have seen the press abuse its freedom?

Possible changes

Information from the Leveson inquiry into the media, resulting from the *News of the World* phone hacking allegations and payments to police officers, will add to the debate about what constitutes a responsible press.

U1 Types of media

Revised

Traditional media – newspapers, magazines, television. All these formats have a declining audience; fewer people are buying newspapers or watching news on the television than in the past. Instead of watching TV programmes in real time, people are increasingly accessing programmes via the internet at times to suit them.

Newspaper	July 1980 sales	July 2011 sales
The *Sun*	3.7m	2.8m
The *Daily Mirror*	3.6m	1.2m
The *Daily Mail*	1.9m	2.0m
The *Daily Telegraph*	1.4m	0.6m
The *Times*	0.3m	0.4m
The *Guardian*	0.4m	0.25m

New media – the development of the internet and related means of communicating are increasingly used by citizens to gather information.

Social media – blogs, Twitter and Facebook are now considered under a separate heading when discussing news. They are called democratic forms of news as they have no censorship. Individuals create or report the news from their perspective. While there is no control over censorship, there are also no filtering mechanisms in regards to truth or accuracy. YouTube is also used as a media outlet, but again items placed on YouTube cannot always be verified.

Possible changes

The Government has had discussions about the regulation of social media and the internet, whether it is possible, and whether it is right to censor in particular circumstances.

Test yourself

Tested

1 What is meant by the term 'social media'?
2 What do you understand by the term a 'free press'?
3 How is the press currently regulated?
4 What issues arise when news is not filtered or carefully checked?

Quick quiz online

Exam practice

Unit 1, Short Course: Section B

a) What is meant by the term 'mass media'? *(2 marks)*

Answers online

Online

U3 Media distortion

Revised

Several issues arise when discussing the concept of media distortion.

● Does the media have its own news agenda? For example, is it running certain types of story so that the public believes that the issue is more important than it might appear?

● What is the role of the media in regard to the formation of stereotypes and labelling groups? For example, the media's use of language and phrases can become the agreed use of the terms – for example, 'hoodies' as a negative description of young people.

● With the current wide range of media sources available to citizens, it is easier to see a range of views and opinions. It is not only UK-based news outlets that are available but many television viewers now have access to US, Russian and Middle Eastern news broadcasters.

Examiner tip

Remember to revise a range of different forms of the media and be able to quote an example of each. When mentioning the media, try to ensure that any case studies you use are recent.

Remember

● Media is more than just newspapers.
● There is a move away from traditional mass media to internet-based media.
● Social media is a force in regard to news and the power of citizens to create their own news agenda.
● Citizens can create their own news agenda via the internet.
● The way citizens access the news and any commentary on events is changing.
● Some media formats give a greater choice and range of views.

Examiner tip

To help your revision, look on the Press Complaints Commission website (www.pcc.org.uk/cases) to study the types of cases it is investigating in regard to media distortion.

U3 Politicians and the media

Revised

In recent years, the media and politicians have become equally dependent upon each other. The media wish to have the latest news and politicians need the media to promote them and their ideas. It is no longer the lengthy speech that gets reported but the sound bite, which is a few seconds long, that will be used on television or quoted in the newspaper. If a politician is concerned about climate change, rather than a detailed analysis and a speech, they visit the North Pole for a 'photo opportunity'.

For politicians during an election, it is vital that they promote themselves and their views through the media. In the UK, the focus is increasingly on the main party leaders. The style of reporting can become presidential, with more concern shown for the leaders, their families and their perceived strengths and weaknesses than for debate about party policy.

Examiner tip

For more detail to aid your revision, look at the biographies of two former prime ministers who had differing relationships with the media: John Major and Tony Blair.

U3 Case studies: how groups use the media to influence others

Revised

The power of the media to inform is immense as is its power to motivate and bring citizens together to make a difference.

Examiner tip

This area of the specification is best revised through the use of case studies. Try to keep your case studies recent, but if they are from the past make sure that they had a major impact.

Case study:

A television programme called *Cathy Come Home* was made for *The Wednesday Play*, a drama on the BBC in 1968. This was the shocking story of a young homeless couple caught in a poverty trap. It led to the formation of the homeless charity Shelter, and also helped to invent an entirely new kind of television drama.

Sir Bob Geldof organised the Live Aid concerts in 1985, which were watched by 1.9 billion people in 150 countries. These events energised citizens to campaign in greater numbers about poverty, and especially the plight of children dying from hunger. The success of these events relied heavily upon their promotion by the media and the media broadcasting the concerts. The concerts raised £150 million.

In 2008, Joanna Lumley, a well-known actress, agreed to support a campaign to help the Gurkas, troops from Nepal who fought in the British army, stay in the UK after they retire. Her father had served with the Gurkas. Her use of the media promoted the cause to the front pages of newspapers and to the top of TV news coverage. Her direct and public contact with politicians and her ability to get answers enabled the Gurkas to achieve their aims.

If you study your local media outlets, you will see examples of how groups and individuals try to involve the media in their campaigns.

Exam practice

Unit 3, Full Course: Section B, Question 6

b) How do pressure groups gain the attention of the media?   *(6 marks)*

Answers online ──────────────── Online

4.1 How effective are the key international bodies in dealing with important international and global issues?

Key terms

Conflict – a state of open, often prolonged, fighting; a battle or war.

Conflict resolution – the means by which conflicts are resolved other than by a military solution. These may include negotiations, arbitration or institution building, which promote the peaceful ending of a conflict.

Human rights – basic rights and freedoms to which all people are entitled.

Human rights abuse – actions taken that are contrary to agreed international charters on human rights.

International conflict – a conflict that involves at least two states in disagreement with each other.

International co-operation – countries working together to achieve a set goal.

International humanitarian law – agreed law in regard to human rights, normally drafted by international bodies, i.e. the United Nations.

U1 The roles of key international bodies

Revised ☐

The United Nations (UN)

- The UN was established at the end of the Second World War. It replaced the League of Nations, which was founded at the end of the First World War to maintain world peace.

- It now carries out many of the functions that the League of Nations had: maintaining international peace, solving international problems and promoting human rights.

- The UN is based in New York where all member countries meet in the General Assembly.

- The decisions that it makes are not legally binding upon its members.

- The Security Council is a smaller body that is part of the UN. It meets to discuss issues and emergencies as they occur. It has the power to pass resolutions, which can impose sanctions or lead to UN troops being deployed. It has five permanent members and another ten that are elected every two years by the General Assembly. The UK is one of the five permanent members alongside the USA, Russia, China and France (the major Allied countries during the Second World War).

- Much of the work of the UN is carried out through agencies working on its behalf (see table below).

- When the UN was established in 1945, there were 51 member countries. In 2011, there were 193. South Sudan joined in 2011.

Examples of UN agencies

World Health Organisation (WHO)	The directing and co-ordinating authority for health within the United Nations system. It is responsible for providing leadership on global health matters, providing technical support to countries and helping to monitor and assess health trends.
The United Nations Educational, Scientific and Cultural Organization (UNESCO)	An agency that contributes to peace and security by promoting collaboration among nations through education, culture, science and communication.
UN AID	An agency that works to improve access to HIV treatment, prevention, care and support.

The European Union (EU)

- The EU was formerly known as the European Economic Community and the 'Common Market'.

- It was established as a result of the Treaty of Rome, 1957, which proposed the creation of a common market for goods, workers, services and capital within the member states.

- There were six founding members: France, Germany, Italy, the Netherlands, Belgium and Luxembourg.

- The UK did not join until 1973 alongside Ireland and Denmark.

- The original aim of the organisation was to improve trade between member countries and build closer links to avoid another world war.

- It headquarters are split between Brussels and Strasbourg.

- It now has 27 member countries, 17 using the Euro as a common currency.

- The EU is now involved in many aspects of the economic life of its member countries.

- It has its own Parliament, which is directly elected by the citizens of the EU.

- Power still resides with the member states, which can still individually veto some new policies.

- All major changes to the functions and role of the EU come into force after a new treaty has been agreed; the last major changes were in 2009 with the Lisbon Treaty.

North Atlantic Treaty Organization (NATO)

- NATO is an intergovernmental military alliance based on the North Atlantic Treaty, which was signed in April 1949.

- The NATO headquarters are in Brussels, Belgium.

- The organisation provides a system of collective defence whereby its member states agree to mutual defence in response to an attack by any external party.

- There are currently 28 member states of NATO, with the most recent being Albania and Croatia, which joined in April 2009.

- The combined military spending of all NATO members constitutes over 70 per cent of the world's defence spending.

The Commonwealth

- Formerly known as the British Commonwealth, this is an association of mainly former British possessions and colonies that are now independent countries.

- Some members were not formerly British colonies but have joined the Commonwealth.

- The Commonwealth aims to develop democratic governance and provides aid and financial support and technical and education support to member countries.

- The Commonwealth heads of government meet annually.

- The Commonwealth Secretariat, an organisation that carries out the plans agreed by the Commonwealth heads of government, has its headquarters in London.

- The Queen is the head of the Commonwealth.

The G7/G8

- The G7 is a meeting of the Finance Ministers of the seven leading industrial powers.

- The G8 is also known as the Group of Eight, (the G7 plus Russia).

- It is an assembly of world leaders who meet annually to discuss global issues.

- Each year, the G7/G8 holds a Leaders' Summit, in which the heads of state and government of member countries meet to discuss and attempt to resolve major global issues.

The G20

- The G20 is also known as the Group of Twenty, and consists of finance ministers and central bank governors.

- It was formed in 1999 to bring together all the important industrialised and developing economies to discuss key issues in the global economy.

Possible changes

- During an economic crisis, look out for the outcomes of G7/G8 and G20 meetings.

- If there is an international crisis, like that in the Middle East during 2011, look at the UN website to find out about its involvement.

- The economic crisis surrounding the Euro relates to the EU, so look at its website for more information.

- NATO is currently involved in Afghanistan, so study its website to understand how NATO forces are being deployed there.

Examiner tip

Ensure that you review the websites of these organisations prior to your exam so that you can refer to any contemporary events in which they are involved.

Websites

www.un.org/en
http://europa.eu/index_en.htm
www.who.int/en
www.unesco.org.uk
www.unaids.org/en
www.nato.int/cps/en/natolive/index.htm
www.thecommonwealth.org
www.g8.co.uk
www.g20.org/about_what_is_g20.aspx

Examiner tip

Each international body has a distinct role. Make sure you are clear about their powers and functions, and whether they are political, economic, military or social. Do they have real power or can they only recommend action? All of them have increasing membership – why do countries wish to join these organisations?

U1 Case studies: international conflict

- The term **'international conflict'** implies a dispute between two or more countries that leads to military action.

- **Internal conflict** is when different factions within a country are fighting.

- **Civil war** is an internal war within a country, which may lead to the break-up of the original country.

You are required to have an understanding of one case study of international conflict.

Case study: Israel and its neighbouring state

One case study that is often used is that of the continuing conflict between the state of Israel and neighbouring states, which dates back to the founding of the state of Israel in 1948. There have been three major conflicts to date between Israel and its neighbouring countries in 1948, 1967 and 1973. This case study has many aspects as it has also involved both the USA and Russia as supporters on either side. There have been several attempts at peaceful solutions and numerous summit conferences. The current plan is for a formal two-state solution, but there are still issues over the detail and differences of opinion within both Israeli and Palestinian political groups. Many see this conflict as one of the reasons for the development of various terrorist groups and terrorist actions.

At the heart of this case study is the basic right of states to live in peaceful co-existence with their neighbours. But where there is disagreement, how is it best to resolve the issues?

Key events in the Arab/Israeli dispute

1947: Britain cannot bring peace to Palestine and turns to the UN. In resolution 181 they agreed to divide Palestine into a Jewish and Palestinian state

1948: War between Israel and her Arab neighbours

1948 –50: 725,000 Palestinians leave Israel, 160,000 remain behind

1956: Suez campaign: the UK, France and Israel seize the Suez Canal in Egypt

1967: Six Day War between Israel and her Arab neighbours

1973: Yom Kippur War between Israel and her neighbours

1978: Israel and Egypt sign Camp David agreement

1993: Oslo Agreement agreeing the principles for a peaceful settlement

Other recent case studies could include the conflict in the former Yugoslavia and the intervention of other countries in Afghanistan or Libya.

Possible changes

If your case study relates to an ongoing conflict, make sure you are up to date in your knowledge prior to the examination.

Websites

http://news.bbc.co.uk/1/
shared/spl/hi/middle_east/
03/v3_ip_timeline/html
www.crisisgroup.org

Test yourself

Tested ☐

1 Why was the European Union established?
2 Why would a country wish to join NATO?
3 How does an international conflict differ from a civil war?

Quick quiz online

Exam practice

Unit 1, Short Course: Section B, Question 5

a) What is the difference between the G8 and the G20?   *(2 marks)*

Answers online — Online ☐

U3 Case studies: human rights abuse

Revised ☐

You should be aware of at least one case study involving human rights abuse.

Case study: genocide in Rwanda

In 1994, Rwanda's population of 7 million was composed of three ethnic groups: Hutu (85 per cent), Tutsi (14 per cent) and Twa (1 per cent). In the early 1990s, Hutu extremists blamed the entire Tutsi population for the country's increasing social, economic and political problems. The Hutu also remembered past years of oppressive Tutsi rule. Many of them not only resented but also feared the minority.

Hutu extremists launched plans to destroy the entire Tutsi civilian population. Political leaders who might have been able to take charge of the situation and other high profile opponents of the Hutu extremist plans were killed immediately. Tutsi and people suspected of being Tutsi were targeted. Entire families were killed at a time. Women were systematically and brutally raped. It is estimated that some 200,000 people took part in the Rwandan genocide. During the genocide, 800,000 men, women and children were killed, perhaps as many as three-quarters of the Tutsi population. At the same time, thousands of Hutu were murdered because they opposed the killing campaign. The film *Hotel Rwanda* is based upon the story of the genocide.

An International Criminal Tribunal was held to hold those responsible to account. This tribunal highlighted the need for a permanent International Criminal Court.

Case study: human rights in China

Amnesty International has documented widespread human rights violations in China. An estimated 500,000 people are currently held in detention without charge or trial, and millions are unable to access the legal system to seek redress for their grievances. Harassment, surveillance, house arrest and imprisonment of human rights defenders are on the rise, and censorship of the internet and other media has grown. Repression of minority groups, including Tibetans, Uighurs and Mongolians, and of Falun Gong practitioners and Christians who practise their religion outside state-sanctioned churches, continues.

Websites

www.hrw.org
www.unitedhumanrights.org/category/reports
www.rwanda-genocide.org

Exam practice

Unit 3, Full Course: Section B

c) Referring to a case of human rights abuse that you have studied, to what extent did the international community hold those responsible to account?

(12 marks)

Answers online ———————————————————— Online ☐

Examiner tip

In order to answer this exam practice question, you need to have detailed knowledge of at least one case study of human rights abuse. Mentioning other case studies where the outcome or impact was different can strengthen your response.

Remember that this is a short essay so you need to plan your response carefully. If we deconstruct the question, these are the key points and possible structure.

1. Identify your case study and mention the time frame.

2. Give a brief account of the background to the case study.

3. What human rights violations took place?

4. How did the international community respond to these abuses, especially the UK?

5. How were those responsible held to/not held to account?

6. What conclusions can you draw from your case study?

4.2 What are the challenges faced by the global community regarding inequality, and how might they be dealt with?

Key terms

Economic system – the way in which a country's business and service sectors are organised, e.g. private sector, public ownership.

Global inequality – the situation whereby the wealth of the world is spread unevenly between countries, leading to vastly different living standards.

Globalisation – the ways in which the economies of individual countries are becoming more closely linked and how, by cutting trade barriers, the world's economy will expand. It describes the process by which regional and national economies, societies and cultures have become integrated through communication, transportation and trade. The phrase 'living in a global village' is used to describe the process of globalisation.

U1 The positive and negative aspects of globalisation

Revised

- The world's economies have developed ever closer links since 1950 in trade, investment and production.

- The pace and scope of globalisation has increased in recent years to involve more industries and more countries.

- The changes have been driven by liberalisation of trade and finance, changes in how companies work and improvements to transport and communications. Consumers of goods like to purchase the latest goods at the cheapest possible price. Producers of these goods wish to manufacture the goods at the lowest price and maintain a profit margin. In order to do so, the producer will produce the goods wherever it is cheapest to source the material or labour.

- There have been losers as well as winners from globalisation. China has been the biggest winner as it has been able to produce goods cheaply. Workers in manufacturing in the western economy, where goods are more expensive to produce, have been the biggest losers.

- There are benefits, but there are also drawbacks to globalisation. A benefit is that consumers get cheaper goods and a wider range of goods to choose from. Drawbacks include increase of mileage involved in transporting goods, and production outside the UK doesn't always benefit the workers who produce the goods.

Examiner tip

When studying this topic, it is helpful to consider your own behaviour as a consumer. Where are the goods produced that you value most – in the UK or in China? When you go out to eat, do you expect a wide range of food that is not just produced in the UK?

Websites

http://news.bbc.co.uk/1/hi/in_depth/business/2007/globalisation/default.stm

Globalisation: some of the benefits and drawbacks

Benefits	Drawbacks
Goods produced overseas cheaply	Loss of jobs at home
Poorer countries able to buy wider range of foreign goods	Poor countries unable to develop their own industries due to imports
Purchase the same goods all over the world, e.g. McDonald's	Restricts development of businesses in the host country
Economies of scale for producers	Small producers/farmers forced to sell at low costs

Possible changes

The Doha Development Round are talks sponsored by the World Trade Organisation (WTO). The most recent round of negotiations attempted to resolve some of the issues relating to liberalising world trade. Carry out some research to find out the most recent position on this prior to your examination.

Examiner tip

- Have a clear definition of globalisation. Do not confuse it with fair trade or ethical trading. Free trade is one component of globalisation.

- While globalisation is traditionally concerned with economic issues, the phrase is also used in regard to cultural issues.

- Be clear about both the advantages and disadvantages of globalisation to consumers, workers in the developed world and workers in less economically developed countries.

U1 The world economic system

Revised

Three types of economic systems co-exist in the modern world: the market economy, the planned economy and the mixed economy. Each has its own advantages and disadvantages.

In a **market economy**, national government plays a minor role. Instead, consumers and their buying decisions drive the economy. In this type of economic system, the concept of the market plays a major role in deciding the right path for a country's economic development. Market economies aim to reduce or eliminate entirely subsidies for a particular industry, the fixing of prices for different commodities and the amount of government regulation. The market economy is associated with capitalism. The leading exponent of the market economy is the USA. Terms such as private enterprise and free market are associated with a market economy.

The **planned economy** is also sometimes called a command economy. Within this type of economy, all the major decisions are taken by government. There is no market that determines inputs or outputs. This type of economy tends to be inflexible in the face of change. This style of economic management was associated with countries that had communist governments.

The **mixed economy** combines elements of both planned and market economies. This system exists in many countries where neither the government nor businesses control the economic activities of that country – both sectors play an important role in economic decision-making. In a mixed economy, there is flexibility in some areas and government control in others. The UK has a mixed economy model, although in recent years the model has become more market orientated.

The economy of a country is also defined by its development.

Least Economically Developed Countries (LEDCs) are mainly non-industrial nations. They tend not to manufacture goods and their residents are usually poor. Another term for LEDCs is Third World nations. There are currently 48 LEDCs including Chad, Niger, Yemen, Nepal and Haiti.

Examiner tip

Revise the key elements of each term. It will help your revision to have an example economy to quote in your response.

Remember

These are key terms relating to economic development. Remember them as groups of terms rather than individually.

Economic systems – planned, mixed and market.

Economic development – MEDC, BRIC, LEDC.

More Economically Developed Countries (MEDCs) are those countries that are rich. These include the UK, Australia and the USA.

BRIC refers to the countries of Brazil, Russia, India and China, which are all deemed to be at a similar stage of newly advanced economic development. This term is used for countries that are not yet fully at the stage of being a MEDC.

U1 Fair trade, ethical trading, globalisation and aid programmes

Revised

Fair trade is about paying producers in the developing world a fair price for their goods so that they can have decent working conditions and local sustainability. By requiring companies to pay a sustainable price for products from the developing world, fair trade enables producers to improve their position and have more control over their lives. The World Fair Trade Organisation is an international body that promotes the aims of fair trade to ensure that producers receive a fair price for their goods. Increasingly, goods such as tea, coffee and bananas are marketed in shops as fair trade products.

Ethical trading is concerned with the rights of workers within the supply chain. There is growing awareness of the exploitation of workers in developing countries who produce goods for wealthy countries. These forms of exploitation can include the use of forced labour, physical abuse and child labour. Ethical trading is concerned with the conditions of workers. It works with employers to ensure that basic human rights are enforced.

Aid programmes: most developed countries give aid to the poorer countries of the world. The UK is committed to spending 0.7 per cent of its national income on foreign aid by 2013. Much aid is organised multilaterally via several countries working together, i.e. through the EU and the UN. Private aid donated by individual citizens is channelled via NGOs (Non-Governmental Organisations) and pressure groups such as Oxfam.

Free trade is about ensuring that each country has a free market where the goods/services of one country can compete equally with others.

Possible changes

A number of citizens in the UK have claimed that we cannot afford to give the amount of foreign aid that we currently have proposed (0.7 per cent).

Websites

www.fairtrade.org.uk
www.dfid.gov.uk

Remember

- Remember that fair trade and free trade have different meanings.
- Remember that fair trade and ethical trading have different meanings.
- Aid can be given via a variety of means, by governments and private citizens.

Test yourself

Tested

1 In which economic category would you place China?
2 Identify one ethical trading issue.
3 Identify two fair trade products sold in the UK.

Quick quiz online

Exam practice

Unit 1, Short Course: Section B, Question 5

b) What are the benefits of fair trade?   *(6 marks)*

Answers online   Online

4.2 What are the challenges faced by the global community regarding inequality, and how might they be dealt with?

U3 Contemporary global economic agendas   Revised ☐

World Bank

This is not a bank in the traditional sense. It is made up of two different development institutions, the International Bank for Reconstruction and Development (IBRD) and the International Development Association (IDA), which are owned by its 187 member countries. The World Bank's aim is to help developing countries by giving them money and technical assistance to improve their education, health and infrastructure in order to help them reduce poverty in their country.

United Nations Conference on Trade and Development (UNCTAD)

UNCTAD was established in 1964. It aims to assist developing countries by bringing them into the world economy. The organisation works to fulfil its aims by carrying out three key functions, which are to:

● be a forum for intergovernmental discussions

● carry out research, policy analysis and data collection for the debates of government representatives and experts

● provide technical assistance tailored to the specific requirements of developing countries.

International Monetary Fund (IMF)

The IMF came into formal existence in December 1945, when its first 29 member countries signed its Articles of Agreement.

● It oversees the international monetary system and monitors the financial and economic policies of its members.

● It keeps track of economic developments on a national, regional and global basis, consulting regularly with member countries.

● It provides loans to countries that have trouble meeting their international payments and cannot otherwise find sufficient financing on affordable terms.

G8 (G7/G20)

Although the G8 is best known for its annual summits, it works throughout the year to tackle important issues such as the economy and climate change. The G8 discusses and creates global policies. Member countries can decide whether or not to support G8 policies.

U3 Case studies: campaigns for global economic issues   Revised ☐

You are expected to have knowledge of at least one campaign and issues relating to one global economic issue, such as free trade, fair trade, poverty, child labour and aid programmes.

Case study: Make Poverty History

Make Poverty History is a campaigning group that wishes to reduce poverty throughout the world. The biggest ever anti-poverty movement came together under the banner of Make Poverty History in 2005.

Great steps have been made since then but the campaign against poverty continues. The group believes that rich countries are blocking a global trade system that would help get rid of poverty in the world. They claim that this injustice will only change if enough citizens across the world call on the governments of rich countries to change their trade policies – for example, at the World Trade Organisation (WTO).

Gordon Brown, the former UK prime minister, acknowledged that the G8 made further concessions in 2005 because campaigners had made debt 'a crucial public issue'.

Case study: fair trade

The recent discussion at the Doha Development Round is the latest attempt at trade negotiations by the WTO. Its aim is to achieve major reform of the international trading system through the introduction of lower trade barriers and improved trade rules. The Round was officially launched in 2001.

Websites

www.makepovertyhistory.org/takeaction
www.wto.org

Exam practice

Unit 1, Full Course: Section B

c) Discuss the impact of any one campaign in regard to a global economic issue.

(12 marks)

Answers online   Online

4.3 What are the challenges of global interdependence and how might they be tackled?

Key terms

Agenda 21 – an action plan of the United Nations (UN) related to sustainable development. The plan was an outcome of the UN Conference on Environment and Development (UNCED) held in Rio de Janeiro, Brazil, in 1992. It is to be undertaken globally, nationally and locally. In the UK each local authority has a Local Agenda 21 plan which links to issues regarding sustainability and recycling. The amount of rubbish recycled is linked to Agenda 21.

Alternative energy – a term used to describe sources of energy supply that are not based upon traditional non-renewable fossil fuels, i.e. coal, oil or gas. Examples include wind, solar and tidal power. These sources of power are renewable and normally linked with low or no carbon emissions.

Climate change – a significant and lasting change in the distribution of weather patterns over periods ranging from decades to millions of years.

Global interdependence – mutual dependence at a global level. One country depends on another country for something and that country may depend on another country, which eventually creates global interdependence. The import and export of goods and services contributes to global interdependence. Certain resources, such as oil and gas, create a global interdependence between countries that produce the resources and those that consume the resources.

Recycling – processing used materials (waste) into new products to prevent waste of potentially useful materials and to reduce the consumption of new raw materials.

Sustainability – using the Earth's resources in a sustainable way, i.e. replacing materials – plant a tree for every one cut down, pay an air tax levy to cover the cost of the plane's carbon emissions.

U1 Case studies: sustainable development

Revised

As a part of the course, you are required to have an understanding of one case study relating to sustainable development. This study can be based upon a local, national or international initiative.

Case study: alternative energy in rural Cornwall

The residents of the village of St Goran in rural Cornwall set up a company called Community Power Cornwall. This company has erected two wind turbines on land at Tregerrick Farm, north of Goran Highlanes in Cornwall, in order to generate community-owned renewable energy.

The villagers raised the money needed from a share offering and they are selling on the electricity the wind turbines produce under the Feed-in Tariff, a government-backed measure to make money from generating energy by selling it back to the National Grid.

A spokesperson for Cornwall County Council has said, 'It is great to see communities taking an active role in developing their own renewable energy schemes.'

The income from the sale of the electricity will go to the shareholders and be reinvested in more renewable energy schemes and community grants.

Websites

North Devon District Council Local Agenda 21 website: www.northdown.gov.uk/template1.asp?pid=680&parent=675&area=4 www.communitypowercornwall.coop/page35g.html

Examiner tip

When revising this topic, you will need to carry out some internet research to find out both what is happening in your local area and what is happening nationally.

Exam practice

Unit 1, Short Course: Section B, Question 5

a) What is Local Agenda 21?   *(2 marks)*

Answers online   Online

U3 Case studies: global interdependence   Revised

You need to understand one case study in depth to be able to consider the concept of global interdependence and how governments can implement policies to bring about improvement. Topics can include climate change, population growth or a world trade issue.

Climate change

According to the UK Government, climate change relates to the increase in the Earth's average temperature since the beginning of the twentieth century and its impacts now and in the future.

Since about 1900, the average near-surface temperature of the planet has increased by 0.75 degrees Celsius and the UK's sea level has risen by about ten centimetres. Further global rises are expected, as well as more extreme weather events such as flooding and drought.

This is a useful area to study as it has many aspects.

● Some people dispute that climate changes are having a negative impact.

● Some countries deny any responsibility and are taking no action.

● Other countries are very active in trying to change their impact upon the climate.

It is an issue in which we all can play a part and try to make a difference.

Exam practice

Unit 3, Full Course: Section B

b) Describe how you could make a difference in regard to a global issue you have studied.   *(6 marks)*

Answers online   Online

4.4 Why should British citizens care about, or be involved in, world affairs?

Key terms

Intergovernmental bodies – international bodies where nations can agree or disagree with the outcome and are not bound by any decisions made. An example is the Commonwealth.

Supranational – international bodies where individual countries hand over some of their power. An example is the EU.

U1 The role of the UK within international organisations

Revised ☐

United Nations (UN)

● The UK was a founder member of the United Nations in 1945. Owing to its status as an Allied power, it was one of five countries that were granted permanent membership of the Security Council. This status gives the UK a right to veto decisions of the Security Council.

Examiner tip

When revising this topic, it is helpful to research each institution prior to the examination so that you can quote recent evidence to support any points you are making.

European Union (EU)

● The UK joined what is now the EU in 1973. It was not one of the six founder members.

● All members of the EU have equal status. Any country has the power of veto over some policy changes.

● For six months at a time, each country occupies the presidency of the Council.

● The UK is often seen as a reluctant member of the EU. During Margaret Thatcher's time as Prime Minister, she fought against further extensions of EU power and negotiated the UK financial rebate.

● Political parties in the UK have often changed their position in regard to the EU.

 – The Conservatives negotiated our membership in 1973, but by the early 1990s the party was split over the EU.

 – The Labour Party was originally opposed to our membership, but under Tony Blair wished to be at the heart of Europe.

 – The Liberal Democrats have always been the most pro-European of all the political parties, but now their attitudes to issues such as Euro membership is less clear.

NATO

● The UK is a founder member of NATO and has the second highest defence budget of members after the USA.

● All UK military planning is based upon our membership of NATO and its joint defence strategy.

● UK forces are made available to NATO for agreed military actions.

● Many military officers are seconded to NATO for training and strategic planning.

The Commonwealth

- Formerly called the British Commonwealth, the Commonwealth is made up of 53 states.

- It was formed in 1931.

- It has its headquarters in London.

- It represents 30 per cent of the world's population.

- The head of the Commonwealth is the Queen. She attends the Commonwealth Games, and on Commonwealth Day, the second Monday in March, she broadcasts to all members.

- The Commonwealth is a voluntary organisation. Its members do not agree to work together in other forums or all vote together (like the UN).

- The Commonwealth has no charter or constitution but the heads of government meet every two years. In 2011 it was proposed that a members' charter be drafted to include a Human Rights Commissioner to monitor human rights.

The World Trade Organisation (WTO)

- Based in Geneva, the WTO was set up in 1995 when it replaced the General Agreement on Tariffs and Trade (GATT), which formed in 1948 when 23 countries signed an agreement to reduce customs tariffs.

- The UK was a founder member.

- The WTO is an international body whose purpose is to promote free trade by encouraging countries to abolish import tariffs and other barriers. It has become closely associated with globalisation.

- The WTO is the only international agency overseeing the rules of international trade. It polices free trade agreements, settles trade disputes between governments and organises trade negotiations.

- WTO decisions are absolute and every member must abide by its rulings. So, when the USA and the European Union are in dispute over bananas or beef, it is the WTO that acts as judge and jury.

- WTO members are empowered by the organisation to enforce its decisions by imposing trade sanctions against countries that have breached the rules.

World Bank

- The UK's relations with the World Bank are decided by the Department for International Development (DFID) and the Treasury.

- Within DFID, the International Financial Institutions department (IFID) and the Global Funds and Development Finance Institutions department (GFDD) help draft UK policy.

- In the Treasury, the International Finance department is responsible for preparing policy advice.

- The UK is the fourth largest shareholder in the World Bank (4.3 per cent).

International Monetary Fund (IMF)

- The top UK representatives at the IMF and World Bank are the Chancellor of the Exchequer and the Secretary of State for International Development. They are known as UK governors to the Fund and Bank, sitting on the ministerial committees, which meet in Washington twice a year to decide on the direction for the institutions.

- The UK is the fourth largest shareholder in the IMF (4.8 per cent); the USA is the largest shareholder with over 16 per cent.

- Following completion of the latest round of funding for the World Bank's International Development Association (IDA), the UK will be the single largest donor to the World Bank.

Websites

http://europa.eu/index_en.htm
www.un.org/en
www.nato.int/cps/en/natolive/index.htm
www.thecommonwealth.org
www.wto.org
www.worldbank.org
www.imf.org/external/index.htm

Test yourself

Tested ☐

1 Identify two international organisations of which the UK was a founder member.

2 To which entirely voluntary international body does the UK belong?

3 If a country is in debt from which international body does it seek help?

Quick quiz online

Exam practice

Unit 1, Short Course: Section B, Question 5

b) Why might the UK Government seek assistance from the IMF?

(6 marks)

Answers online — Online ☐

U3 Case studies: UK involvement with an international body

Revised ☐

You are required to look at one key current debate relating to the UK and an international body. The term 'debate' is used rather than 'dispute' so you have a broad range from which to choose.

In relation to many bodies, the UK works collectively with the EU and together they present a common policy.

Possible case studies to research include:

● the UK and Euro membership

● the role of the UN in regard to the Middle East, the IMF and the current world economic crisis.

The topic you select should be contemporary and fit into one of the three headings: 'the UK and the European Union', 'the United Nations' or 'another supranational organisation'.

Examiner tip

Ensure when revising that your case study is up to date. Look at the relationship between those involved. If there is a debate there are at least two differing points of view so make sure you are aware of the range of views on your chosen issue.

Exam practice

Unit 3, Full Course: Section B

b) Referring to a case study, explain a current debate involving the UK and the EU.

(6 marks)

Answers online — Online ☐

4.5 How are international issues influenced? The citizen's voice in the global village

Key terms

Global citizenship – a Global Citizen (as defined by Oxfam) is someone who:

- is aware of the wider world and has a sense of their own role as a world citizen
- respects and values diversity
- has an understanding of how the world works economically, politically, socially, culturally, technologically and environmentally
- is outraged by social injustice
- participates in and contributes to the community at a range of levels from local to global
- is willing to act to make the world a more sustainable place
- takes responsibility for their actions.

Global village – used to refer to the fact that with the ability to travel and the speed of news and 24/7 media, the world is becoming a smaller place as far as how quickly the impact of something elsewhere is felt in the UK.

Non-Governmental Organisation (NGO) – organisations that are not government controlled but work closely with government. They tend to provide services for those in need rather than formally campaign or take any form of direct action. An example would be the International Red Cross.

Participation – taking part in society through formal processes such as voting or standing for election, or informal actions such as volunteering or joining community groups.

Pressure group – a group of people working together to achieve an aim. It is not a political party in that it does not put candidates forward for election. An example would be Make Poverty History.

U1 Pressure groups and NGOs involved in international campaigning

A number of pressure groups and NGOs were established to campaign in regard to international issues.

- Some groups like the Stop the War Coalition developed as a response to specific events – in this case, the war in Iraq.
- Others, like Oxfam, developed as a response to poverty.
- Greenpeace was established to campaign in regard to environmental issues.

NGOs such as the Red Cross are more general in their aims, often providing specific services such as medical assistance.

These organisations campaign in the same ways as UK-based pressure groups and use the same methods (see pages 15–16). In order to develop an understanding of this topic, you will need to research a range of groups to understand the nature of their work.

Possible changes

Ensure that the campaign or the issue you are investigating is current. Many organisations that start by campaigning in regard to a specific issue often develop into broader coalitions.

Examiner tip

When revising this topic, it is helpful to visit the organisations' websites so that you have current information about their campaigns.

Websites

www.greenpeace.org.uk
www.redcross.org.uk
www.stopwar.org.uk
www.makepovertyhistory.org
www.oxfam.org.uk
A directory of NGOs from across the world:
http://ngo.epha.org

U1 How can individuals effect change in regard to an international issue?

Revised

Using the case studies you have already researched, focus on the role of the individual citizens in bringing about change. This will show the power of citizens working together to bring about change.

Individuals themselves have started campaigns that have become international. Rebecca Hoskin of Modbury, Devon started a local campaign about the use of plastic bags which has now become international.

In 1985 Sir Bob Geldof and the Live Aid concerts led to a focus on world poverty and Third World debt. This led to the development of the Make Poverty History campaign.

Amnesty International actively encourages well-known individuals to become involved in its campaigns. To find out more use the weblink opposite.

Websites

www.looktothestars.org/charity/19-amnesty-international
www.live8live.com

Test yourself

Tested

1 What does NGO stand for?
2 Identify a UK-based group that campaigns on international issues.
3 Outline one method a citizen could use to influence an international issue.

Quick quiz online

Exam practice

Unit 1, Short Course: Section B, Question 5

a) Identify one international NGO. *(2 marks)*

Answers online

Online

U3 How do different groups influence international issues?

Revised

You may wish to use the same research you have undertaken for the short course for this section of the full course. The Make Poverty History campaign meets the criteria for both exams.

For the full course you need to investigate how the campaign influenced the international debate in regard to the issue. The Make Poverty History campaign has involved international music concerts, mass demonstrations, lobbying of foreign leaders and campaigning. It has achieved the setting of international targets in regard to debt reduction.

Another case study could be on the Global Campaign for Education.

> **Examiner tip**
>
> Make sure that you revise your chosen campaign and quote up-to-date information about its work and achievements.

U3 How can information from pressure groups, voluntary groups and NGOs be used in public debate and policy formation?

Revised

- Many governments and other national and international bodies allow pressure groups and NGOs access to allow for the exchange of ideas.

- Within the European Union this process is formalised whereby the EU has to consult registered groups before issuing policy proposals.

- Where groups do not have informal or formal access, they have to try to use the power and influence of the media, ask their members to support campaigns and lobby on their behalf or use celebrities to promote their cause.

- The Live Aid campaign demonstrates the power of the use of celebrity and the influence of the media.

Exam practice

Unit 3, Full Course: Section B

a) To what extent has Make Poverty History achieved any of its aims? *(6 marks)*

Answers online ─────────────── Online

Answers

Topic 1.1 What factors make for effective 'active citizenship'?

Test yourself page 19

1. Examples include: Free speech, freedom of association, freedom to vote.

2. A citizen who participates in community life, uses opportunities to participate in the democratic process and has the necessary skills to be able to attempt to bring about change.

3. *Votes at 16, Fathers for Justice, No to Identity Cards.*

4. An individual or group of people, or an organisation or body that a person wants to influence in regard to a decision.

5. Pressure groups campaign in regard to one issue or a limited range of issues. Political parties stand for election to win office at a local and national level and campaign on a wide range of issues.

Topic 1.2 Who can make a difference?

Test yourself page 25

1. A means of communicating to a large number of people at the same time. Examples are newspapers, television, film and the internet.

2. Most newspapers are owned by public or private companies so they can put forward any views. The Government regulates television and ensures that it is politically impartial (does not favour one political party over another) and covers the views of all the major political parties in its reports.

Topic 1.3 How and why are Citizenship issues relevant in the workplace?

Test yourself page 32

1. Examples include: racial, sexual, age, religious and disability discrimination.

2. Your rights are protected in the same way as a full-time permanent employee if you work sufficient hours and for a reasonable period of time.

3. No, they don't have to change the dress unless it is faulty or isn't as described, but most retailers do operate a policy allowing you to change goods.

Topic 2.1 What are the roles of Parliament and Government?

Test yourself page 38

1. In 2011 the Conservative and Liberal Democrat parties made up a coalition government in the UK.

2. National parties from Wales, N. Ireland and Scotland – SNP Scottish Nationalist Party, Democratic Unionist Party (DUP) or Plaid Cymru.

3. A Public Bill is one proposed by the Government. A Private Members' Bill is one produced by a backbench Member of Parliament.

4. This is a stage when a group of MPs study the detail of a proposed law line by line and make proposals for amendments.

5. Traditionally the three major posts in the cabinet after the Prime Minister are: the Chancellor of the Exchequer, the Foreign Secretary and the Home Secretary.

Topic 2.2 How can citizens participate in democratic processes, particularly elections and voting?

Test yourself page 47

1. Examples include: Voting systems used in the UK; First Past the Post (FPTP), Party List, Additional member system (AMS).

2. Single Transferrable Vote (STV).

3. Non Proportional: First Past the Post, Additional Vote; Proportional: STV, Party List, AMS.

Topic 2.3 The origins and implications of diversity in the United Kingdom

Test yourself page 52

1. Where people have an unreasonable dislike of others. This is not evidence-based, as in for example, cases of racial prejudice.

2. The United Kingdom is made up of England, Scotland, Wales and N. Ireland.

3. It is the only part of the UK to have a land boundary with another country – the Irish Republic and its Government must be made up of elements representing the differing communities in N. Ireland.

4. Examples may include: Fairness and justice; the ability to have equal access to the law; the ability of the press to express a range of views; openness

to people who are oppressed in their own countries. Many of these values are not solely linked to Britain and are often seen as universal values that all countries should have.

Topic 2.4 Ethnicity, identity, community life and promoting cohesion

Test yourself page 58

1. Examples include: *The Race Relations Act 1965, Equal Pay Act 1970, Equality Act 2010.*

2. *The Equality Act 2006* established a new government body called the Commission for Equality and Human Rights, which brought together numerous former bodies to form one new body to deal with all issues relating to human rights and equality.

Topic 3.1 What are my rights and responsibilities as a British citizen within a broader framework of human rights?

Test yourself page 66

1. Cases against individuals who are accused of human rights abuse.

2. The United Nations Declaration of Human Rights, written after the Second World War, sets out the key human rights that countries must follow.

3. Rights of UK citizens include: right to vote; trial by jury; right to an education; freedom of expression.

Topic 3.2 How are citizens' lives affected by the law?

Test yourself page 70

1. Examples include: A civil case normally doesn't involve a jury; a civil case involves a dispute between individuals while a criminal case is a case between an individual and the state; civil cases normally involve a settlement by a financial award, while a criminal case can involve a custodial sentence.

2. Examples include: The right to buy a lottery ticket; get married with their parents' consent; work full-time; choose their own doctor (GP).

3. Ensure you select an age-related right and give a reason for your choice. An example response: Currently you have to ask your parents if you want to get married at sixteen. I think sixteen-year-olds should be able to get married at sixteen

without their parents' consent. You already gain a lot of rights at sixteen and are able to work full-time and have sexual relationships, therefore you should be allowed to marry without having to ask for permission.

4. Example response for the idea: The right to vote should be lowered to sixteen from eighteen. Sixteen-year-olds are already considered responsible enough to have many rights, including the right to work full-time and to get married, and pay taxes like everybody else. I think it is important sixteen-year-olds have a say in the way the country is run.

Example response against the idea: Most sixteen-year-olds are not really interested in politics. Many are still at school and are not mature enough to make political decisions at that age.

Topic 3.3 How effective is the criminal justice system?

Test yourself page 75

1. The current age of criminal responsibility is 10.

2. Examples of aims of sentencing: To punish the offender; deter others; protect the community; reform the offender; provide reparations to victims of crime.

3. Restorative justice brings offenders and their victims together so that people who commit crimes make amends and understand the impact of their crimes.

Topic 3.4 Why does the media matter and how influential is it?

Test yourself page 81

1. Social media refers to the use of web-based and mobile technologies to turn communication into an interactive dialogue between people using applications such as Twitter, Facebook and blogs.

2. A 'free press' means that the press are free to publish stories and are only restricted by the laws that affect every citizen. There is limited or no government control of the press.

3. The Press Complaints Commission currently regulates the press; this is an industry-based form of self-regulation. At the time of writing in 2011, this system is currently under review following the *News International* phone hacking controversy.

4. Issues that can arise could include: inaccuracy, distortion or political bias. Incorrect financial news could impact on the decisions of financial markets.

Topic 4.1 How effective are the key international bodies in dealing with important and global issues?

Test yourself page 87

1. The European Union originally began as the European Economic Community (EEC) in 1957 as a result of the Treaty of Rome. It was known informally as the Common Market. Initially it was intended to draw the economies of the member countries closer together and thereby prevent a further European war.

2. A country would join NATO for defence from non-members, in effect to strengthen its military forces.

3. International conflict involves two countries fighting each other. A civil war takes place within a country between differing groups based within the country.

Topic 4.2 What are the challenges faced by the global community regarding inequality, and how might they be dealt with?

Test yourself page 91

1. China is one of the countries which make up the acronym BRIC (Brazil, Russia, India and China) which are all deemed to be at a similar stage of newly advanced economic development. China is quickly becoming a more economically developed country.

2. Examples include child labour or the standard of working conditions for all employees (for example, wages, hours, rest periods and health care).

3. In the UK a large number of fresh fruit carry Fairtrade labels, also goods such as chocolate, coffee, and cotton.

Topic 4.3 What are the challenges of global interdependence and how might they be tackled?

Test yourself page 95

1. 'Alternative energy' refers to the use of non-fossil renewable fuels such as wind, wave and solar power.

2. Advantages of recycling include: Reuse of goods; less environmental damage by not having to produce replacement goods; creates less waste by avoiding disposal of items; creates jobs in the recycling trade; saves non-renewable resources.

3. The United Nations estimated that, on 31 October 2011, the world's population would reach 7 billion. This highlights that sustainability is an issue because every economy has a need for natural resources, and the world's growing population puts a strain on these resources. It is therefore important to try to replace resources such as trees that are being cut down, and develop new technologies to help reduce consumption of resources. Food and other resources including clean drinking water are becoming scarcer.

Topic 4.4 Why should British citizens care about, or be involved in, world affairs?

Test yourself page 98

1. Examples include: The United Nations, the IMF and NATO. The UK was not a founder member of the EU.

2. The UK belongs to the Commonwealth, which is a voluntary organisation.

3. If a country were in debt it seek help from the International Monetary Fund (IMF).

Topic 4.5 How are international issues influenced? The citizen's voice in the global village

Test yourself page 100

1. NGO stands for Non-Governmental Organisation – any non-profit organisation which is independent from government.

2. Examples include: Amnesty International campaigning in regard to human rights and Oxfam in regard to poverty.

3. Examples include: Joining a pressure group; lobbying an MP or MEP; writing letters to the media; forming a pressure group.